BOOKS

TO HELP YOU GROW YOUR FAITH

365 daily *Devotionals* FOR WOMEN

*E*MBRACING *H*OPE AND *H*EALING

FINDING FREEDOM IN GOD'S LOVE

Claudio de Castro

Catholic writer

ISBN: 9798335649414

To those who seek holiness
with their lives.

To my beautiful wife, Vida.
To my children who bring me so much joy:
Claudio Guillermo,
Ana Belén,
José Miguel,
and Luis Felipe.
To my mother and my dear brothers:
Henry and Frank.
And to my precious granddaughter,
Ana Sofía.

This book belongs to:

Me

anne Catterine Sare

……………………………………………………………………………………

Do you know who Claudio is,
the author of this devotional for women?

CATHOLIC BEST-SELLING AUTHOR

Claudio de Castro writes books to help you grow your faith. He supports the reader on their journey with their Christian faith.

Claudio is a husband, father, grandfather, and a contemporary Catholic author. He is a globally recognized writer. He declares himself "a friend of Jesus in the Tabernacle." He comes from a Jewish family with many traditions. His grandfather was named Abraham Moises and there are several rabbis in his family. Claudio is a devout Catholic. He won the highest literary award in his country, Panama, The Ricardo Miro Award, and has been a contributor to the Worldwide Catholic Agency Aleteia., publishing weekly articles as well as in other Catholic media outlets, newspapers, and Catholic radio programs.

He draws inspiration from his daily experiences and his regular visits to Jesus, a prisoner of love, who awaits us in the Tabernacles. He is passionate about supporting readers with his words and his over 200 books on personal and spiritual growth, published on Amazon. His purpose is to bring Jesus to others and provide them with comfort, hope, and peace.

Dive into a transformative journey with the new Catholic book collection by bestselling author Claudio de Castro! Elevate your spiritual growth with profound insights from these compelling reads. Uncover the secrets of faith, love, and salvation as you immerse yourself in Claudio's rich narratives. Join the community of enlightened readers and embark on a path to spiritual enlightenment.

If you're interested in finding Catholic books on spirituality, we would recommend Claudio's books, which cover a wide range of topics in spiritual growth. He is author of numerous books including: The Invisible World, the Tabernacle, the Great Secret: How to Obtain What We Ask from God, my Guardian Angel.

Don't miss out – secure your copies now and let the wisdom of these Catholic treasures ignite your soul!

"They say that a man is not truly a man until he hears his name from the lips of a woman."

Antonio Machado

"I thank you, woman, for the very fact of being a woman! With the intuition inherent to your femininity, you enrich the understanding of the world and contribute to the full truth of human relationships."

Juan Pablo II, Letter to Women, 1995

ACKNOWLEDGMENTS

To the women who have been an example to me and those who, with their kindness and wisdom, have influenced my life: my mother, my grandmother "Mamita," and my second-grade teacher who taught me to love Jesus in the Tabernacle, the Franciscan sister María Ávila.

To my daughter Ana Belen, my sunshine, my moon, my star; and my beautiful granddaughter Ana Sofía, for the enthusiasm with which they encourage me to write.

To Vida, my wife, my companion, friend, guardian of my secrets, who understands, cares for, encourages me, and brings me joy. It was she who, when I was 50 years old, said to me:

"You have a dream to fulfill, to be a writer. Leave everything and pursue your dream; I support you."

I raise a toast with this book to 39 wonderful years of marriage, 4 children, one daughter-in-law (Mafe), and one granddaughter, all extraordinary; and to being able to share our lives together.

"Not as I,
but as You;
not when I;
but when You.
If this is Your will;
it is also mine."

Blessed
Maria Concepcion
Cabrera de Armida

"I love it! It's a book that fills the soul... Each day a short reading that reminds us we are not alone and that we should always see the wonders that God gifts us, even in the smallest things. We can use it year after year to grow our spirituality and relationship with God."

"I don't usually write reviews about anything, but this book changed my life from day one of reading it."

"I love this book, especially if you feel like you don't have much time to read. Each day of the year has a little reflection, and it doesn't take more than 2 minutes to read."

"It truly inspires you and makes you think. I keep it by my bedside so I can read the reflection of the day before going to sleep or upon waking up. Very beautiful book. 100% recommended."

Don't worry.
Everything
will be fine.
Just trust.
God will do
the rest.

Thank you so much.

In your hands you have my first devotional for women, and perhaps my most important book, which in Spanish has been a great success among readers of Catholic self-help and spiritual growth books. Years of study, Biblical readings, writing, and publishing books are condensed into this magnificent work for your spiritual and personal benefit. You will find Bible quotes, meditations, personal experiences, and a means to increase our faith, our vocation to beatitude and holiness, the longing to love, service to others, and our prayer, through which all paths are opened.

Did you know that many women have the opportunity to rise from bed each morning with enthusiasm, resilience, and optimism? What a beautiful awakening knowing because of your faith that it is true that God says to you, "Do not be afraid, I am with you." These are women of faith, with a strength tested in every way, and with a purpose to fulfill, because they are certain of being loved by God, from eternity. I know several women like this.

I am Claudio de Castro, a Catholic author, and that is what I do every day: I rise knowing that I will do what I am passionate about and I will teach you how to achieve it as well, how to persevere, strengthen your faith, and find a purpose in life. With God in the midst, each dawn becomes a new and extraordinary adventure. You discover that life, despite so many difficulties, is worthwhile, a gift given to us, a present from God. Every day I ask myself: "What will the good God have prepared for me today?" Life makes sense if you keep God in the middle of everything you do.

With 5 minutes a day of reading and daily reflection you will feel amazing. My wife says it's a "lifesaver”, so you don't drown. You will be more capable of overcoming difficult situations, facing adversity, and living the life that God, as a loving Father, prepared for you. God wants you to be happy and has promised you a Paradise, where we will live eternally and in peace. The Glory of God is so dazzling that we can barely imagine it. The apocalypse (22) gives us an idea of what the hereafter will be like: "The angel showed me the river of the water of life, clear as crystal, flowing from the throne of God and of the Lamb. In the middle of its street, and on either side of the river, was the tree of life, bearing twelve kinds of fruit, yielding its fruit every month; and the leaves of the tree were for the healing of the nations. And there will no longer be any curse; and the throne of God and of the Lamb will be in it, and His bondservants will serve Him; they will see His face, and His name will be on their foreheads. And there will no longer be any night; and they will not have need of the light of a lamp nor the light of the sun, because the Lord God will illumine them; and they will reign forever and ever."

Friends and readers have accompanied me over 15 years in this extraordinary apostolate of the written word and I feel honored and grateful. I thought a lot about you when writing this book. It is a way to honor and thank Jesus ALIVE, a prisoner of love in the Tabernacles of the world, where you often find Him abandoned. Jesus, my childhood friend. It is also my contribution to readers from many countries, a way to compensate for their support of our evangelizing project. Therefore, I hope this book is special and accompanies you in your growth for a year, filling you with optimism, encouraging you to follow God's paths. Does what I do have any merit? Very little. They gave me the easiest, writing about God and the Gospel. The merit is in living it, setting an example with our lives. That is the meritorious part. Merit is had by the woman who decides on holiness, despite adversity, and dedicates her life to doing good, quietly, without making noise or being noticed. May God grant us that gift born of love, of humility, when we forget ourselves, to think of others. Knowing this, every time a reader thanks me because one of my books changed her life, or gave her a purpose, or made her discover God's love, I refer her to the Tabernacle. "Thank Jesus, He did it all, what is really important is his work. I just write."

Let us be guided by this thought of Saint Josemaria Escriva: "Dream and you will fall short." We were born of faith, the desire to serve God, hope, and much encouragement. Did we need anything else? Because that's all we had. I am aware that, without your prayers, your words of encouragement, and your constant support - acquiring my books, sharing them, commenting on their reading with reviews - we would not have reached where we are, with more than 250 titles printed and digital on Amazon, many published in 4 languages, selected among the most recommended in their categories of Catholic books, with several Best Sellers. I take a moment to reflect, I read the Bible: "He who loves Me will be loved by My Father, and I will love him and will disclose Myself to him." (John 14:23) And I understand... We lack being God's abode. If God lived in us, we would do the things that please Him. We would have courage and charity. We would go through the world with a pure heart. We would look with the gaze of Love, a gaze of charity, a gaze of brother. Let's be brothers. Without hatred or disputes. I will try. Are you encouraged? Since I started this apostolate, every day is a new adventure with God. I can see the world with new eyes and rediscover creation, grateful for so much love. I discovered that God is patient, merciful, tender, just, and waits for us. He is Love and loves us. He is Father and always listens to our prayers. With this book I make a necessary stop on the road. I just turned 66 years old. God's path is full of stops and surprises to discover. You stop at a crossroads to gather strength and start a new adventure in His Love. I was thinking of these words of Saint Paul to the Galatians: "But as for me, I will never boast about anything except the cross of our Lord Jesus Christ. Because of that cross, my interest in this world has been crucified, and the world's interest in me has also died." If God gives me a choice again, I will go wherever He takes me. I will unfurl the sails of my soul and let His Holy Spirit blow. Life is a gift and a mystery, but also extraordinary, always worthwhile. In the face of these wonders, I cannot help but exclaim, "Thank you! How good you are, Lord!"

WHAT IS A DEVOTIONAL

The word 'Devotion' comes from the Latin 'Devovere' which means 'having made something sacred'. And devotional is a word that comes from "devotion, love, contemplation". If you search on the Internet, you will find that "It is a special time we dedicate to connect and strengthen our communion with God." Jesus taught us by His example, withdrawing to pray and be alone with God. In this book for today's woman, from teenagers to seniors, we have recorded many personal experiences and stories shared by my readers, which have had an impact on many lives. It is a loving encounter with God that transformed their lives forever. Knowing they are loved fills them with peace, strength, and hope. They continue to face the same problems, but they confront them with joy, peace, and serenity, knowing that this world is passing and not our true home. Difficulties confront us and strengthen us. The Bible in 1 Corinthians 10:13 assures us that God is with us and takes care of us: "No temptation has overtaken you that is not common to man. God is faithful, and he will not let you be tempted beyond your ability, but with the temptation he will also provide the way of escape, that you may be able to endure it." We are pilgrims heading towards heaven. At the end of your days, you understand that the only thing that matters is saving our immortal souls and all those we can.

This book with 365 meditations, one for each day of the year, will inspire your life. It is a DEVOTIONAL, and it contains prayers and devout practices. "It allows you to have peace, serenity, and a practical and simple encounter with God." Its content: Normally, devotionals include novenas, prayers, Bible verses, devotions, and teach you to trust, pray, and live in God's presence. I wanted to do something different, to go further and help you in your relationship with God, sharing my experiences, faith experiences, and so many testimonies that I receive from my readers. If you ask me what this book is about, what it will teach you, one word is enough: "LOVE." Love sums everything up. We do not need anything else. The Sacred Scriptures remind us: "I give you a new commandment, that you love one another. Just as I have loved you, you also should love one another. By this everyone will know that you are my disciples, if you have love for one another." (John 13:34-35) This is a devotional that had been requested for a long time. It contains 365 daily inspirations for women, very useful and that will make you feel better.

I carefully chose the meditations that have touched more lives among all my books. It will not take you more than 5 minutes to read and reflect on them. I selected them with a prayerful spirit, from among all my books, to give them to you in this book. Each meditation will serve to remind you that we are body and spirit, and a wonderful eternity awaits us alongside God. You will be able to spend time alone with God and with yourself. You will be able to deepen your relationship with God and apply the inspirational content of each page in your daily life. You will have in your hands a daily thought to fill you with enthusiasm, restore your faith, strengthen you spiritually, and regain the certainty of a God who walks with us and loves us from eternity.

Now, why read a Catholic devotional? To begin with, it will do you much good, strengthen your spirit, and allow you to live an extraordinary life. With God in the middle, everything is extraordinary.

If you are one of those who think "you can't take it anymore," that the great challenges of this world are defeating you, you should read it; it will be a guide and inspire you. Don Bosco said that nothing does as much good to the soul as a good book of spirituality. This is one. It will help you to remain in the presence of our Lord and God, good and eternal Father, and to discover his voice in the Holy Scriptures.

When to read it? You have many options.

• In the mornings when you wake up. With each word, you will receive a boost of optimism to start the day.
• At noon after lunch. It will serve as necessary food for your soul, which you must also take care of.
• At work before starting the day. It will assist you in putting yourself in God's presence. Its reading and reflection will strengthen and clarify your thoughts.
• On family outings it will accompany you, and you will be able to read it aloud for the benefit of those around you.
• At night before bed, thanking God for the wonderful day you have had.

I hope this Catholic Devotional enriches your life. There are many reasons to read it and share its reading. I will give you 10 reasons to have this wonderful book of spiritual growth in your hands.

Those who have read it tell us:

1. It's simple yet profound words awaken and revive our faith.
2. It gives us encouragement to overcome life's difficulties.
3. It helps you understand your purpose in this world, discover why we are here.
4. Every word reminds us that we do not walk alone on the path of life. God walks with us and cares for us.

5. It strengthens you spiritually.
6. It allows you to discover God's gift, his goodness, his presence in your life.
7. It will make you feel spiritually strengthened again, optimistic about life.
8. It will clarify your mind so that you can find a better solution to your problems.
9. It will show you a simple path to holiness.
10. And finally, it will help you spend moments of peace, leaving aside the problems and difficulties you face in your daily life.

You can start reading it today, keep track of each devotional, or open the book at random. However, you choose to read it, it will be fine. Blessings are for you; you only have to reap them. You will find 365 thoughts to encourage you and remind you that we are never alone, that life is an immense, extraordinary gift that is worth living. If you decide to seek God, you will be able to hear him say excitedly when he touches your heart, "With everlasting love I have loved you." (Jeremiah 31)

One thing is certain: from the day God touches your heart, a desire arises in your soul to know more about Him. It is an inexhaustible feeling, to know Him more, to spend hours before the Blessed Sacrament, and to feel again that immense Love that floods our souls. You long for His Peace, which gives us strength to charge against the world and silence shame. That Peace that is like a fortress that protects us, impels us to be heroes of God, and to be holy. Doing what is right is not always the easiest. It brings consequences, but it is worth it. If you trust in God, He will be by your side and in the end... everything will be fine. I put this Catholic devotional with beautiful reflections that I wrote for your benefit and personal and spiritual growth into your hands. I ask God to help you increase your faith and renew your hopes and trust in His love. With this book, you do not need a table of contents, so you will not find one.

Lord God and my father.
Act in my life as it pleases you.
That I may be for you
and you for me.

WHY DID I WRITE IT?

Some years ago, I used to chat with a priest over the internet. He was very ill and often disappeared, only to resume our conversations weeks later. I knew he was dying, so one day I asked him, "What is it that you have liked the most about your priesthood?" On my computer screen, there appeared only one word:

"CONSOLE."

I never heard from him again. It struck me as extraordinary to meet someone who dedicated his life to consoling those who suffer, those who have experienced loss, or are going through painful affliction, and I wanted to do the same with my books: to bring comfort.

Each book has been born from a personal experience. I write about family, my difficulties, the search for God, I answer my readers' concerns, and I share the daily experiences of a father. This book you hold in your hands will show you new paths to overcome pain and misunderstanding. I have followed these paths myself and proved that they work.

In the morning, I wrote some reflections to use in the book. It was a list of things we can do to improve our lives. My wife Vida was beside me, and when I finished, she jokingly added, for me to include it as well: "And hug my wife more." So, I stopped what I was doing and hugged her. It's the small details, the simplest ones, that make you happy.

Don't think that because I write these books my life is simpler than yours. I've thought that everything that happens to us has a purpose. Things don't happen by chance. God prepares our paths for something better. "Is this a joke?" you might say to me. "Can't you see what I'm going through?" With our poor humanity, we can't understand it at this moment. Who could? But later everything will make sense.

God often meets us when we least expect it. He rescues us from the meaningless life we lead and invites us to be better, to follow Him. Recently, I heard about this Spanish young man who hung out with the wrong crowd, smoked marijuana, and spent thousands of dollars on parties. One day his mother invited him to accompany her to the Escorial Monastery. There they prayed the Holy Rosary with other people. Suddenly, God made Himself present and flooded him with His grace. In that moment, everything changed for him. Every time he passed by a Church, he felt God calling him strongly to enter and visit. He let himself be seduced by Divine Love and began frequenting the Churches. Currently, he is a seminarian and will soon be a priest.

Who can understand God's ways? Not I. I no longer want to understand, but to trust, to abandon myself in His loving Fatherly arms, to let Him pamper me like a mother does her small child.

As I write to you, a great pain overwhelms my soul. Suffering is part of our lives. I used to tell people, "How can you call yourself a disciple of the crucified if you have not suffered?" And now I have had to live it. I must learn to be a disciple. To offer my pain. To accept God's will.

The truth is that no one likes to suffer. It makes us vulnerable. However, it also elevates us. It raises our souls to unsuspected places. The effect of feeling that we can no longer go on is immediate. When all human resources have failed, and you are lying on the ground, you lift your gaze to God, pleading.

He is your only hope, the only one who can help you in such moments. In these days when my life has been so altered by difficulties, suddenly I have understood that carrying this cross can be a blessing, a gift from heaven. It has forced me to turn my gaze to the Creator, made me pray more and with more fervor. It has shown me that when we have humanly tried everything possible, the only thing left for us is God. It has moved me to reread books of spirituality and watch movies about the lives of saints. I am in search of answers, wondering what to do, why this is happening to me, how I can move forward. I meditate more. Sleep less, but I spend time in His presence, immersed in His Love. These questions, along with my many concerns, fade away as the days go by. Now I just want to look at the cross... To be with Him, to embrace Him.

The great mystics used to have a preference for contemplating the cross, meditating on it, on the sufferings of Our Lord. They said that on the cross we can learn the fundamental, that in it we will find the key that will open the doors of heaven.

Gabriela Mistral has a poem full of tenderness about the Cross. Do you know it? Let me share a fragment: "In this afternoon, Christ of Calvary, I came to beg you for my sick flesh; but, seeing you, my eyes go back and forth from my body to your body with shame. How can I complain about my tired feet, when I see yours torn apart? How can I show you my empty hands, when yours are full of wounds? How can I explain my loneliness to you, when on the cross raised and alone you are? How can I explain that I have no love when your heart is torn? Now I do not remember anything, all my ailments fled from me. The impetus of the prayer I brought with me is drowning in my begging mouth. And I only ask not to ask you for anything. To be here next to your dead image and to learn that pain is only the holy key to your holy door." The poem is true. How can we complain when we see Him on the cross? In these conditions, I have sat by the window in my room, taken my laptop, and started writing. I felt calm, serene, filled with that wonderful presence of God.

COME, HOLY SPIRIT

Before we continue, let us ask God for His blessing with a prayer born from the heart. Praying will always bring us great spiritual benefits. The Holy Scriptures tell us a historical moment that happened after the apostles prayed. Read it, and you will understand why I insist that we pray, at all times, insistently and fervently. "After they prayed, the place where they were meeting was shaken. And they were all filled with the Holy Spirit and spoke the word of God boldly." (Acts 4)

Let's begin with a prayer to the Holy Spirit, it is the oldest hymn known. "We are weak but the Spirit comes to our aid. We do not know how to ask or what to ask for, but the Spirit asks for us, without words, as with groans." (Romans 8)

Let us ask God to pour out His Power upon us and ignite our hearts with love and grant us the 7 gifts of the Holy Spirit, which He reserves for those who ask. The Catechism of the Catholic Church describes them: "wisdom, understanding, counsel, fortitude, knowledge, piety, and fear of the Lord." And then it explains how they help us:

"They complete and perfect the virtues of those who receive them. They make the faithful docile in promptly obeying divine inspirations."

Let us pray:

Breathe into me, Holy Spirit, that my thoughts may all be holy. Move in me, Holy Spirit, that my work, too, may be holy. Attract my heart, Holy Spirit, that I may love only what is holy. Strengthen me, Holy Spirit, that I may defend all that is holy. Protect me, Holy Spirit, that I may always be holy.

365 DAILY REFLECTIONS

to Build Confidence and Faith

You are everything to God.
It's just that you haven't
discovered it yet.

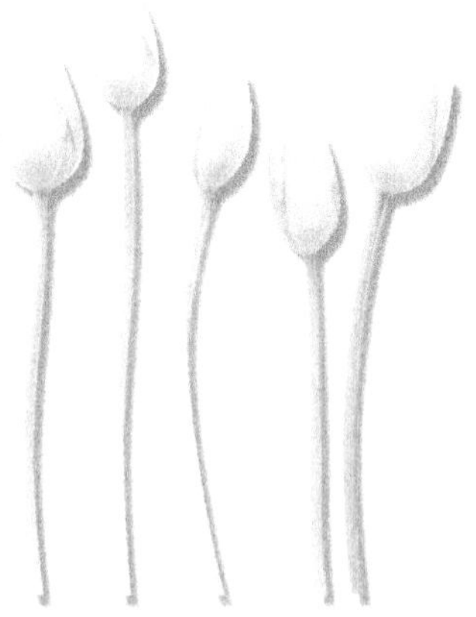

I love starting my devotionals with
an invitation to enthusiasm and the joy of living.

~1~

Today is the first great day of your new life, a life in God. Come on, get up! Cheer up! Rise up!

This morning I remembered with excitement when I was a child and Jesus was my neighbor in a chapel across from my house on 9th Street, Roosevelt Avenue in the city of Colon. I loved visiting Him in the mornings before going to school. Knowing He was there deeply impressed me. I used to peek out the window of my house to greet Him. Jesus was my neighbor and became my best friend, my childhood friend. I realized that the secret was grace, the purity of the soul. In grace lies all that is sacred and pure. Grace would allow God to dwell in me, to be united with my soul. I would have to raise my eyes to God and offer him a new life. And I could be with Him, live in his loving presence, regain my childhood friend. I had to achieve grace, have a pure soul again. That was it! The soul was too heavy, chained to so many sins, and could not fly, rise to God. I prayed so little and thought less about spiritual life. All this had remained in unfulfilled purposes.

This happens to many of us. We have our soul so full of sins that it is like carrying a sack of very heavy stones that prevent us from running, advancing, dreaming, praying, living, meeting God. Some carry a dead soul and keep God away from them, endangering their eternity, eternal salvation. But that won't happen to you. We are going to change starting today. We can change. God awaits us at the end of the road. Today everything will be wonderful for you. We start a new, different life. You have so much to offer to God, to those around you. Surely you smiled and thought, "What happened to this one?" I don't even know. At this stage of my life, there is something inside me that moves me to search. I need to know why many things happened. I have so many concerns. "What does God want from me? Why did this or that happen to me? Why me? What should I do?" For now, I will fill myself with sweet hope, I will be motivated, something good has to happen. Resolve to start over, go through the world being a sign of contradiction. Yes, this will be an exceptional year in your life as a woman. A year that will change your way of seeing things and those around you. To everyone who asks you how you are doing, you will answer, "Excellent."

You are a very special woman. Even if you fall 100 times and are lying on the floor, you will get up 100 times. You have the strength to do it. You will find the answers to your questions. And you will be happy.

"Lord, now I will seek You, let me find You, feel You close, be with You, believe in You and obey You. Guide my steps. Wrap me in Your Love."

~2~

I haven't always been a good friend, even though Jesus is always ready to listen to us, fill us with abundant graces, and comfort us. I was looking at a picture of Jesus. His face looked sad and desolate.

"Who did this to you?" I asked.

"You did," He replied. "The souls of poor sinners sadden me greatly. Yours, especially. Look at the state it's in."

Suddenly, I saw myself as I truly am, with my many flaws and sins. I was horrified. I had thought I was good, that I did good deeds, that I had merit for writing about Jesus. Yet, my soul appeared sick, with dark, disgraceful stains, and a foul odor.

The next day, I hurried to confess and cleanse my soul.

"Better?" I asked, looking at His picture.

"Much better," He replied.

Despite these experiences, I fall again. But I also rise again because I know Him now. I know He is merciful and good, always waiting for me with outstretched hand, as a friend and a brother.

Change is quite an adventure. It requires struggle, perseverance, and it's not easy. I know this well from my own experience. "This is going to be harder than I thought," I smiled to myself. "I'll have to trust in God and try harder," I told myself as I began my journey of conversion and yearned to draw closer to God.

He doesn't make the path easy for you, but He offers an immense reward that makes all your efforts worthwhile. He gives you the strength and grace you need and shows you the path you must follow, what you must do. For those starting over, everything seems confusing. We don't know how to take the first step, what to do. A feeling of joy overwhelms us; we know there's no turning back, that God awaits us, that it's the best choice.

I was determined to improve, to do everything for God, to live in His presence. And I had no idea how to do it. An overwhelming force propelled me and elevated my thoughts toward the Father. I desired to start anew. I had promised God. It was an adventure; I was preparing to climb God's mountain. The good God placed many obstacles in my path, perhaps to test me or strengthen me.

I am naturally not very humble and stubborn, and I wouldn't back down. I moved forward, one day at a time, very slowly, like someone crossing a dense jungle without being able to see the horizon.

Days passed, and I didn't understand what was happening. I had decided to live for God, and it seemed to me that God was doing nothing for me; on the contrary, He made my life harder. I lost my job, with four children and many debts. I didn't understand anything. I felt the need to start reading books on spirituality. I began by buying the lives of the saints. I avidly read everything that came into my hands, as if time to do so were so short that I could never finish a book. I started visiting Jesus in search of answers. I felt that He looked at me from those Tabernacles with infinite tenderness and smiled sweetly at me.

"My little Claudio," He said to me, "Do not be afraid. I am with you."

~3~

FAITH

The greatest grace God has given me is faith. I've thought about this many times, and now I understand that throughout my life He has always been present. He was with me when I took my first steps, when I went to school for the first time, when my father died in my arms while I spoke to him about the wonders he would find in Paradise. God has always been with me and with you. Don't you realize it? He delights in us, loving us, spoiling us, giving us what we need to live. He is constantly wooing us. He shows us glimpses of heaven. He fills us with graces. He does the impossible so that you may discover His loving presence in your life and love Him.

A soul in love does not fear. It accepts everything gladly. And it surrenders itself into the hands of God. I read about the life of a young Catholic, a martyr of the Spanish Civil War. What serenity. What peace. Just before they shot him, he bravely exclaimed:

"Wait a moment! I want them to know that I forgive them!"

Our strength comes from the Lord. Only from Him. That's why it is worthwhile to seek Him, to know Him, to love Him. Today is a good day for you to return to God. Are you weak? Cling to God and you will emerge as a victorious woman of faith, empowered.

God gave you purity of soul and heart. It is a treasure. Do not trample on it. Have you lost it? Do not be afraid. A good sacramental confession will help you restore your friendship with God.

Our God is unlike anything we could think or imagine. He is kind and good, merciful, patient. "The Lord is compassionate and gracious, slow to anger, abounding in love... He forgives all your sins and heals all your diseases." He likes to go slowly with us, according to our steps. He lets the wheat grow with the weeds so as not to harm the wheat. Patience. The day will come when He will separate the good from the bad. For now, there is an opportunity to save ourselves. God is like the good gardener who knows where to prune the dry branches, those that do not bear fruit.

HAVE YOU EXPERIENCED IT?

You feel a great emptiness, a huge and profound hole in your soul that you cannot fill. It fills you with fear, anguish, loneliness, and a desire to always be busy, doing something with your free time. If only you knew that it is such an easy void to fill and achieve personal peace again, a life purpose that fills us with happiness. In those moments, one word is enough, one name, one Father: "God." Some voids are so deep and profound that only the immensity of God can fill them and surpass them.

I'll give you a biblical advice:

"Keep the faith and a good conscience,
not like some who disregarded it
and shipwrecked their faith."

(1 Timothy 1:19)

~4~

"Faith is the realization of what is hoped for, and evidence of things not seen".
Hebrew 11

Do you have faith? That faith that moves mountains and with which nothing is impossible to achieve. Do you find it hard to have faith, right? You must ask for it insistently and plead to Jesus: 'Increase our faith.' A woman who has faith knows that without faith it is impossible to please God... 'for whoever would draw near to God must believe that he exists and that he rewards those who seek him.' (Hebrews 11:6). A woman of faith always accepts God's holy will, which is perfect; she knows that everything that comes from God is for her own well-being and that of her loved ones. She surrenders herself into His loving hands. She knows that what Pope Benedict XVI said is true: 'Whoever lives in the hands of God, always falls into the hands of God.' A woman of faith knows that in the end, everything will turn out well. But what is a woman of faith? How can we define her? On the internet, you can find a beautiful definition that does her justice: 'A woman of faith trusts in God and faces adversity with hope.'

Our God is the God of opportunities. He is the God of Love and reconciliation. He is our Father. You must have the experience of God. That moment when God makes Himself present and you allow Him to dwell in you. You enter into another world; the gates of heaven open for you. God shows you glimpses of heaven to console you. I have always imagined this fleeting experience like walking through a beautiful forest in darkness, not knowing where you are going, but with the certainty of a calling. Suddenly, a ray of light illuminates the sky and allows you a brief vision of the wonders around you. It is so beautiful what you see. You are overwhelmed, longing for the experience to repeat itself. It almost always happens the same way. Suddenly, you understand. Time stops around you. You realize who you are and who He is. You see Him in all His majesty and a deep sorrow for your sins emerges from your soul. The least you want to do is offend such a good God, who at that moment calls you 'Child.' All He desires is to show you the way that leads to His Love. You see yourself as you are, with your faults and virtues. What you could have done and didn't want to. You understand all the potential we must do extraordinary things, promote goodness and mercy. It's too much for one moment and you don't fully understand it. God lovingly consoles us and says, 'Do not be afraid. Here I am.' And He floods you with a love so great, immense, that it overflows. It is so much that you cannot contain it. In that moment, the world around you changes. Now you see them with the eyes of love. You have that gaze of mercy that the world so desperately needs. You would like to embrace them all, love them all. Leave everything and follow God.

A woman of faith is virtuous, full of admirable qualities. She teaches us by her example. A woman of faith always loves first and spreads love wherever she goes.

~5~

"I pray, I ask for the conversion of my husband and my children, and nothing happens. What should I do, Claudio?" This is often asked by kind-hearted women who read my books. The answer is very simple. "Be a woman of faith and persevere in your prayer. And if you lack faith, ask God for faith and wisdom, and He will grant them to you. With faith, you can move mountains.

A woman of faith moves mountains, and adversity never makes her doubt. She is courageous, self-assured, joyful, and kind. Give it a try. Have faith. You will emerge strengthened to overcome adversity, sure of yourself.

- Cultivate a life of prayer.
- Read the Bible, meditate on the Word of God.
- Attend Mass and receive Communion.
- Do good to everyone you can.
- Treat everyone with joy and kindness.
- Have confidence, the certainty that you are not alone, God is with you and loves you.

And when you ask God for something, do it like little innocent, pure children who approach their parents and ask for what they desire, and these, moved by so much love, give them what they ask for if it is for their well-being.

Imagine one of your children always coming to you out of convenience, asking for money. When you give it to them, they leave ungratefully. Now imagine one of your children always seeking you because they love being with you. They enjoy your presence. They love you. They need your good advice. They sit beside you, listening to your stories as if hearing them for the first time, with great interest. And they tell you how much they like them. And they constantly hug you and tell you they love you.

How did you feel in both cases? God is a Father, and He is love. He resents the distance and abandonment of His children. He loves it when we show Him our love, through our actions, words, and thoughts. If you dare to take the first step, I assure you, God will do the rest. What truly matters. When you allow God into your life, everything changes. God carries you in the palm of His hand, and nothing bad can happen to you. This is what is called 'holy abandonment.'

"But how can I learn to trust? It's so hard for me." The key is to know and cling to His Promises. They are in the Bible. You must know them, especially this one: 'Ask, and it will be given to you' (Matthew 7).

Ask and you will receive. It's true! And if you want to trust, go to the Tabernacle and ask Jesus to teach you to trust.

The things I tell you, I haven't read them. I live them every day, I have seen them in hundreds of people who have chosen God. And they have started to see miracles. It's incredible. God is alive and loves you and is your Father. He is a God who loves to spoil His children. You can't imagine how much He enjoys guiding your steps. When you truly begin to trust, the insecurity you feel, the fears that overwhelm you will disappear. God will make Himself present, like the father of the prodigal son who ran to meet his son returning home, embraced him, and showered him with jewels.

Don't worry. Everything will be fine. God loves you. You are special to Him. Trust in God!

~6~

Theodore ("Ted") Robert Bundy was an intelligent, charismatic person, a great seducer, a man who could easily convince anyone. He's not the type of person you would want to encounter. He was also a serial killer, cruel, sadistic, perverted, disturbed. In the early hours of January 15, 1978, at 3:00 a.m., Ted Bundy broke into a sorority house at Florida State University. He carried a baseball bat as a weapon in his hands. He entered a room and brutally killed two young women. Thirsty for blood, he went to another room to find another victim.

With the bat still bloody, he opened the door to the third student's room, saw her sleeping, and holding a rosary in her hands. At that moment, he felt an invisible force pushing against him, preventing him from entering. Instantly, he dropped the bloody bat and fled in terror. That bat provided evidence for investigators to capture and convict him for his many crimes. The young woman woke up, paralyzed by terror. She asked to speak with a priest and told him what had happened. She also mentioned that before going to the University, she had promised her grandmother to pray the Rosary every night to honor the Virgin Mary and seek her maternal protection, and that night she fell asleep praying the Rosary. Life is curious; years later, that same priest spiritually assisted Ted Bundy when he was on death row, hours before his execution, and asked him about the events of that night. "I tried to enter the room to kill that girl," Bundy said confusedly. "A mysterious power that I do not understand prevented me. That force did not let me enter the room to kill the young woman, and that strange force also threw the bat out of my hands. That's why I fled."

There is another even more surprising story about the power of the Holy Rosary that I always relate in my books. The Church remembers the episode and it is documented by historians and doctors. It is known as "the Miracle of Hiroshima." It is 1945, August 6th. The Japanese city of Hiroshima has just been attacked during World War II. The United States dropped the atomic bomb Little Boy from a B-29 bomber named Enola Gay. Over 70,000 people were instantly pulverized. Four German Jesuit priests survived the radiation from the atomic bomb. There is a photograph taken hours after the explosion that is striking. Everything is devastated, pulverized, and amidst so much destruction and death, a church stands intact. When interviewed, the priests said they are accustomed to praying the Rosary and living the teachings of the Virgin at Fatima. Over the years, I have seen many miracles received by people with faith who prayed fervently to God for their help. I have also received hundreds of impactful stories from my readers who tell us their adventures in faith, real stories about the power of prayer that have always impressed me. The Rosary is a Biblical prayer, as its prayers mostly come from the Bible, and it is Christ-centered because we follow the steps and life of Jesus in each mystery. My grandmother in Costa Rica taught us by example to pray the Rosary. Have you experienced something similar? I am Catholic and I am not ashamed to pray the Rosary. How about you?

~7~

"... In this you rejoice, although now for a little while you may have to suffer through various trials, so that the genuineness of your faith, more precious than gold that is perishable even though tested by fire, may prove to be for praise, glory, and honor at the revelation of Jesus Christ."

(1 Peter1, 6-7)

I met a person who for years lived estranged from God. Nothing mattered to him. Greed drove him. He was immersed in business, never prayed, and lived in disbelief. The quantity of money he could amass each day was all that mattered.

One day adversity struck, he lost everything and became desperate. Unsure of what to do, a friend advised him to make a change, suggesting it would do him good to read the Bible and understand what God wanted from him. He found one tucked away in an old piece of furniture and retrieved it. The first words his eyes landed on were this promise:

"Commit your way to the Lord; trust in him and he will act. He will make your vindication shine like the light, and the justice of your cause like the noonday sun." (Psalm 37:5-6)

He felt it was providential, not a coincidence; it was as if God himself was speaking to him, and he looked up to the sky with gratitude. He began to pray and read books on spirituality. Gradually, he regained his lost faith. In time, he also recovered his business and multiplied his possessions, but this time it was under the loving protection of God, not clinging to them. Money became a means to do good, not an end. He dedicated a good portion of his earnings to charitable works. He helped anyone he could, attended Mass, and most importantly, he was happy.

Now he tackles all his activities with such enthusiasm that it surprises everyone. He is a different person, unrecognizable. Always smiling, joyful, content, and kind. God knows how to transform our hardened hearts. We may call it adversity, difficulties, or problems, but it is his extraordinary pedagogy that transforms our lives.

~8~

It is said that a boy had prepared for his First Communion, and the good priest wanted to test if he was ready. He pointed to the Tabernacle and asked, "Who is there?" The boy, with the simplicity typical of his age, first pointed to the cross and said, "There seems to be God there, but He is not," then he pointed to the Tabernacle; "There, on the other hand, God is, although it seems that He is not."

My family, on my father's side, is Jewish; my grandfather was named Abraham Moses Frank. Since I was a child, I have been to the synagogue for family events and some Shabbat, and to the Church because of my faith. It is a privilege to be Catholic.

My life has revolved around the Tabernacle, and since I was a child, Jesus has been my best friend. Now as an adult, I love visiting Him, spending time with Him, telling Him that I love Him. I used to live in Colon, a coastal province of Panama, and in front of my house, the Servants of Mary had their residence with a beautiful chapel containing a Tabernacle. I would peek out of my house window and shout, "Hey, hello, Jesus!" I have no doubt that Jesus is present in every Tabernacle, alive. I have witnessed clear miracles.

Saint Alphonsus once said, "If people would only go to the Blessed Sacrament to seek remedy for their troubles, they would not find themselves as desolate as they are." This morning, my wife and I visited Jesus. A lady approached me, "Mr. Claudio, I want to thank you for your words on Radio María and your books. Thanks to you, I have discovered the living presence of Jesus in the Tabernacles, and now I visit Him daily. Before, it was difficult for me to stay five minutes; I tried to see Him with my eyes, but I only saw the Tabernacle and the lamp of the Blessed Sacrament. One day I asked Him, 'Open my eyes,' and now I see Him with the eyes of my soul so clearly. I spend over an hour with Him, praying, showing Him my love, and in return, He fills my soul with tenderness and peace."

She made me realize the need to speak more in this book about Jesus in the Blessed Sacrament, His throne, and His prison, the Tabernacle. And that's what we will do. We must know Jesus more to love Him more. Believe me, from the Tabernacle, Jesus will change your life.

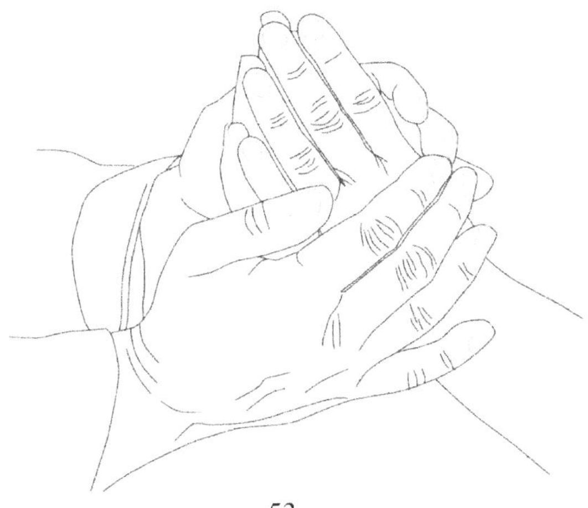

~9~

On that sunny June morning, I found myself in the outer hallway of the National Shrine of the Immaculate Heart of Mary in Panama. A few steps away was the oratory with the Blessed Sacrament hidden in a beautiful bronze Tabernacle.

As I have mentioned before, the Tabernacle is where the priest keeps the consecrated holy host, which has not been consumed during Mass. It is Jesus, and He is ALIVE. Periodically, I glanced towards the oratory and prayed silently.

With permission from the parish priest, I had placed a small table outside the church displaying my books on spiritual growth. Those who approached the table, for some reason, would confide in me about their lives and difficulties. I would gift them a book and encourage them to speak with Jesus in the Tabernacle, assured that He would listen to them and provide the graces necessary to continue life's challenging journey.

From where I stood, I would occasionally return my gaze to that Tabernacle and greet Jesus with affection and respect. By noon, exhausted from the heat, I complained irritably to Him: "Lord, I want to go home. I could be out for a walk with my family, yet here I am, seated. Tell me if this is worthwhile."

Without waiting for an answer, I began packing up the books to leave. Just then, an elderly lady emerged from the chapel where the Tabernacle was housed. I remember her well—short, with a broad smile on her face and white hair. She walked with short, brisk steps down the hallway. When she reached the table, she abruptly stopped, turned towards me, and said resolutely, "It is worth it, Mr. Claudio. You must stay." She didn't wait for me to say anything and continued on her way. Her words left me stunned. I followed her and caught up with her at the exit. "Excuse me. Why did you say that to me? I was already leaving." "I don't know," she replied candidly. "Ask the one who is in the Tabernacle. It's between you and Him." With that, she walked away.

At that moment, I didn't know it, but God had arranged an encounter later that afternoon that would change my life and my perspective on life.

I returned to my post in the church hallway and reflected on what had just transpired, looking perplexedly towards the Tabernacle. I smiled at Jesus and said, "You are something else. You know all the tricks." I endured the sweltering heat willingly, knowing who was keeping me there, although I still didn't know why.

Around three o'clock, I was distracted while rearranging the books and didn't notice a sweet elderly lady standing in front of me, observing me. "Good afternoon," she said.

I looked up and smiled kindly. "Would you be willing to listen to the story of an elderly lady?" "For a beautiful lady like yourself, I am always willing," I replied. "I'm listening." And so she began her remarkable tale:

"I am 89 years old. When I was 15, I became pregnant. In those days, it was a family tragedy. Everything was based on what society would say about our family. Ultimately, it would have been a major scandal. My mother kept me locked up for the nine months of my pregnancy. During that time, I did not see sunlight. She told everyone that I was abroad studying languages.

"When the day of delivery arrived, I gave birth to a beautiful, radiant girl. She filled my soul with joy, hope, and new emotions. Only a mother knows what it feels like when they place your child for the first and last time in your arms.

Everything was arranged for her to be given up for adoption. They placed her in my arms so that I could gaze upon her, caress her beautiful face and hair, and kiss her for the first and last time. I remember her very well. I have clung to her memory. Her infantile gaze, pure and innocent, her little arms waving, touching my face, her pink lips, and her wonderful baby smell were engraved in my memory. They took her away abruptly, and despite my pleas, I never heard from her again. Since that day, every night I cry inconsolably and pray for my daughter, my beloved daughter whom I love more than my own life and whom I will never see again in this world."

Her story shook my soul. How could something like that happen? How does one endure such pain? I didn't know what to say. Out of charity, I maintained a solemn silence. She looked at me gently and smiled faintly. At that moment, thinking about her unspeakable suffering, I dared to ask, "I can't imagine what you've been through. How have you coped? How do you live with so much pain? How do you forgive what they did to you?"

She turned her gaze to the Tabernacle and pointed towards it. "He has given me the strength. Because of Jesus alive in the Tabernacle, I have been able to forgive those who took my daughter away from me. I have found refuge in faith, fervent prayer, and my visits to Jesus in the Tabernacle. Every time I can, I visit Him. I kneel at the feet of the Blessed Sacrament and ask Him to let me rest in His Most Sacred Heart. Without His help, I would never have been able to move forward. Without His love and peace, life would have been impossible for me. I have found the strength to live with dignity through prayer and the consolations He has poured into my soul."

In those sacred moments, she was one with Jesus. And she knew it. That's why she could say, like Saint Teresa of Jesus: "God alone suffices." She needed nothing more to be fulfilled. She knew she was loved from eternity, and this gave her the strength to continue despite her tremendous pain. At that moment, I recalled these words from Scripture: "But whoever is united with the Lord is one with him in spirit." (1 Corinthians 6:17)

Her words deeply moved me; they resonated profoundly within my soul. Her tragedy surpassed the threshold of pain any person could endure. I had many questions, but out of charity, I remained silent. At that moment, I felt the desire to embrace her, to encourage her to continue. She looked so fragile, vulnerable. All I could think was, "Thank you, Jesus, for loving us so much, for helping her to live and forgive and find peace."

Since then, whenever someone with a broken soul tells me their story, I remember that scorching hot afternoon and that defenseless elderly lady, and I realize that few things can surpass such suffering. Most importantly, one can forgive everything, live with dignity, and find the desired peace. Throughout the year in my devotional for women, we will speak of that trust, strength, and faith that can withstand anything.

~10~

"In the Lord we hope; he is our defense and our shield..."
(Psalm 33:20)

We are not alone. God walks with us, beside you, within you. I understood this on Sunday during Mass. Like you, I am not exempt from difficulties. I face them daily; they are part of life. Since then, I have been pondering on this. "We are not alone." I searched in my Bible for God's paternal voice telling us, "Fear not, for I am with you" (Isaiah 41:10). And the reassuring words of Jesus: "...I am with you always, to the end of the age" (Matthew 28:20). Then I understood that I had no reason to worry. Nothing bad can happen if God is with you. Those I have met on this journey, who yearn to live the Gospel, have begun with tenderness. Suddenly, their souls are filled with a tenderness they did not know before. They no longer despise the poor or turn away from them. They listen and do not allow them to leave empty-handed, without a word of comfort.

They have discovered a mystery. They have found Jesus. Almost without realizing it, devout prayer wells up in their lips, and they feel the need to go to a solitary place and speak with God. In that moment, spontaneous joy springs forth from the depths of their soul alongside an inexplicable happiness. It is the joy of being with Him, through Him.

~11~

"In that moment, Jesus met them on the way and said, 'Peace be with you.' The women came up, embraced his feet, and worshiped him." Matthew 28:9

God is a vast, endless ocean, and we are like small vessels seeking to drink from it. It's an impossible task for our frail humanity. Yet, we can have a small knowledge of God by experiencing His love. This has happened to many I know. They love, and the world is different for them. Now, they can forgive easily. They let go of material things and share what they have. They always carry a word of comfort, a hug, a smile. They realized that in God, everything is abundant. There's no need to hoard for tomorrow; they will never lack anything because they have the Creator of all—both visible and invisible—as their father.

After this beautiful experience, they begin to journey the Way in awe, still impacted. They seek silence to hear God. They strive to attend daily Mass to be with Him. And they cherish moments of reflection, meditating on these beautiful truths they are discovering. This knowledge of God and the living presence of Jesus in the Eucharist is a gift given to us, a glimpse of the wonders that await us in Paradise.

~12~

Recently, I was driving my car and remembered that at the National Sanctuary of the Heart of Mary, they had the Blessed Sacrament exposed. So, I veered off my route to stop and greet Him. "You are God," I said. "You created all things. But You reveal Yourself in a small piece of bread. Why can't we see and recognize You in all Your majesty?" Then, in response, a passage from the Bible came to my mind: "Six days later, Jesus took with him Peter, James, and John and led them up a high mountain by themselves to pray. And he was transfigured before them, and his clothes became dazzling white, such as no one on earth could bleach them. And there appeared to them Elijah with Moses, who were talking with Jesus. And Peter said to Jesus, 'Rabbi, it is good that we are here. Let us make three tents, one for you and one for Moses and one for Elijah.' For he did not know what to say, for they were terrified." (Mark 9:2-6) My Jesus, what would happen if we saw You as You really are? Surely, we would also be terrified, not knowing what to say or do. Your divinity is too much for a simple mortal. How good You are to show Yourself so simply and humbly, in something familiar to us, something we do not fear; and that we can confidently approach You. "Truly, you are a God who hides himself, O God of Israel, the Savior." (Isaiah 45:15)

~13~

"The manner of Christ's presence under the Eucharistic species is unique. It elevates the Eucharist above all the sacraments and makes it 'the perfection of the spiritual life and the end to which all the sacraments tend" (CCC).

I don't have to go to holy places to be with you. I encounter you in the Tabernacle. It happens to me that I feel your presence in the Blessed Sacrament; I know you are there, alive, seeing and hearing me. I approach calmly, in peace, serene, as if I were in the midst of my family, knowing that you love me. I feel comfortable when I am with you, Jesus. I don't see you as the relentless Judge who will come to judge the nations, but as the Good Friend who has stayed with us to give us eternal salvation. You are my best friend since childhood, and I am grateful for that.

"The Church and the world have a great need for Eucharistic worship. Jesus awaits us in this sacrament of love. Let us not spare time to meet him in adoration, in contemplation full of faith and open to repairing the serious faults and crimes of the world. May our adoration never cease." (John Paul II)

~14~

I used to spend the summer holidays at my grandmother's house in San José, Costa Rica. In the afternoons, we would sit down to have coffee and eat still-warm rolls, spread with delicious homemade jam. Afterwards, my grandmother would recline on her bed with the rosary in her hand. I would watch her slowly, methodically, recite the mysteries one by one. She did it with such naturalness and beauty.

Grandmothers are great teachers. Perhaps that's why I always carry a rosary with me. I learned to lose the fear of what others might think of me. And from experience, I know that we must overcome the fears we carry within. Monsignor Escriva de Balaguer had already said it: "Lose the fear of calling the Lord by His name - Jesus - and of telling Him that you love Him". To which I added: "Fear of living as a true Catholic. Fear of going against the world. Fear of what others think of us. Fear of being told that it's unmanly, or that we are fools. Blessed fools who walk through the world hand in hand with Mary."

To love Mary is to love Jesus.

You acknowledge that you resemble Jesus because you love His Mother. Indeed, we cannot please Jesus if we do not love Mary. It's as if Jesus reminds us: "He who honors my mother, honors me." Do you want to belong to Jesus? Be of Mary. All saints have been great devotees of the Virgin. And to all of them, she has blessed them with her protection and affection.

~15~

"The Virgin Mary is our spiritual mother, our mother in heaven, never forget that. She watches over you, over us, and takes care of us. We must imitate the saints in everything, especially in their devotion to Mary, and turn to her in our afflictions to ask for her motherly protection and to love Mary. Devotion to the Ever-Virgin Mary is something that has characterized them all. Do not hesitate to turn to the Virgin and ask her to intercede with her son Jesus for you. Did you know that his first public miracle was at the request of his mother? Saint Bernard left us this beautiful prayer to receive from the Virgin her protection and comfort in times of affliction, when temptations afflict us and when we go through difficult times and do not know what to do. I recommend you copy it and always carry it with you. 'Remember, O most gracious Virgin Mary, that never was it known that anyone who fled to your protection, implored your help, or sought your intercession was left unaided. Inspired with this confidence, I fly to you, O Virgin of virgins, my mother; to you I come; before you I stand, sinful and sorrowful. O Mother of the Word Incarnate, despise not my petitions, but in your mercy hear and answer me. Amen.' Where Jesus is, there is Mary. In the Eucharist, in the heart of man. This is a mystery that confuses many. Personally, it fills me with joy, and I love to think about it. Jesus, the Good Shepherd, has an exceptional mother. The most beautiful of all mothers. And the best part is that she is also our mother."

~16~

"I have a beautiful painting of the Virgin Mary in my house - a friend told me - I have placed a small picture of Jesus next to her image. I like to greet them daily before going to work. To feel them as part of my family. And to feel myself also part of them. One day I looked at the Virgin and with filial affection I said to her: 'Hail Mary!' And it seemed to me that she smiled at me approvingly and that Jesus, by her side, also smiled at me. I stopped praying and Jesus stopped smiling. I prayed again and his smile returned. I wondered what that meant and deep within my soul I felt that voice: 'When you honor my mother, you honor me.' Should I imagine it? Love is not imagined, nor seen, it is felt and lived. Loving the mother of Jesus has become a great conflict for many people in recent years. For my part, I love the Virgin Mary, the Immaculate Conception, and I don't mind being a cause of contradiction. I say it from the heart: 'I am of Mary.' She is my mother. I would like to praise her daily, with that poem by Saint Alphonsus: *'Do you know what I want, sweet Mary? My star, I want to love you.'* Since I was little, she has taken care of me and has given me endless signs of her love. I experience her presence in my life with tenderness. And when I face a conflict, I visit her in a chapel near my work and approach her with emotion and great confidence because I know that a mother always listens to her children, no matter how bad they may be. Mary is not different from other mothers; she is even better."

~17~

The example of the Virgin Mary opened for us an inexhaustible path to holiness, purity, and chastity. Through her, saints have flourished in the world. Saints as human as you and I, each living a full life, difficult, with sacrifices, but also with heavenly joys. All of them true lovers and disciples of Jesus. I feel particularly moved when I read about Teresa of the Andes and how she lived from a young age, sure of her vocation, showing us the path of holiness. 'Mary must be my mirror,' she wrote. 'Since I am her daughter, I must resemble her and thus I will resemble Jesus.' Recently, I had a surprise. A new priest. I had never seen him before. Tall. Kind-hearted. With a deep voice. Just seeing him, I thought, 'This is a man of God.' I knew within myself that I was not mistaken. The Our Father he recited was so deliberate and meditative that it made you feel as if Jesus himself was praying it. The moment of communion arrived. I lined up like everyone else. And suddenly I began to sing softly, 'From heaven is Mary, the mother of God...' And I sang and wondered why, as I rarely do this. When the mass ended, the priest said, 'Let's give a song as a gift to our heavenly mother, for today is her day.' And we all sang, 'Hail, Hail, Hail Mary...'

I couldn't hold back. Then I understood. I felt tears welling up in my eyes. 'Mary, how sweet is your name.'

~18~

Visit Jesus, tell Him everything, He will help you. Look at what a beautiful encounter with Jesus a reader has sent me.

~19~

"I am thirsty for God, for the God of life." Psalm 42:3

"I have discovered that everything becomes clear as you draw closer to God, as you decide to live in His presence. It's like climbing a mountain; as you ascend, the horizon becomes clearer and more beautiful. We climb God's mountain, seeking His love, listening to His sweet call: 'Here I am.' The world is thirsty for God, and God is thirsty for our love."

~20~

You can't imagine the happiness I carry within.

I have resumed receiving daily communion. On the outside, I am a serene, distracted Claudio. There are few signs that something wonderful and extraordinary is happening within me.

Suddenly, I smile. It's spontaneous. It's hard to contain the joy, and rightfully so.

To have Jesus with me. To be a living Tabernacle. To know Him as my friend.

Do you understand my reasons now?

~21~

Today I went to receive communion. With each step, a joy welled up in my soul. I looked around and noticed everyone chanting this beautiful melody: 'So close to me, so close to me that I can almost touch Him.' You can't imagine how much reality was in that song. That's exactly how I felt: 'so close to me.' And I understood. Finally, I could understand! 'To find wisdom, the knowledge of God, you must love more. You cannot comprehend Love if you do not love.' It was an indescribable moment, almost magical. You couldn't decipher if you were in heaven or on earth, or if both fused in that splendid instant. 'What are you doing to me, Lord?' I asked Him, 'Everything that used to excite me has disappeared. And now, only You interest me. You have turned my life upside down.' I returned to my seat, pensive. I realized that in that fraction of a second, that brief encounter with God, my life had changed. It would never be the same. Curiously, no one around me noticed. It was an invitation to the greatest thing you can imagine. God dwelled in me, in all of us, and invited us to Love. For a moment, I could understand how glorious, magnificent, and unique God is, and yet He is loving, simple, transparent, merciful, pure, and gentle. Now, each passing day, the temporal things lose the appeal they once had. I no longer strive for what I possess. I have other dreams. There are higher, loftier things that seem unreachable and now captivate me and move me to conquer them. No one but God can fulfill my hopes and give meaning to my life.

~22~

While writing this book, I met Maria Jesus, a cousin of my wife Vida. I did something curious; I promised her that I would mention her in the book and asked her to share some of her many experiences with God. The next day, she sent me this beautiful testimony:

'I believe it is impossible to know God and not fall in love with Him. It is impossible not to love Him from the depths of our being, even with imperfect love, for we are imperfect. When that Love is born, it envelops you in such a way that it breaks all the chains around you and truly sets you free. It is a liberating love that begins with an 'ineffable infatuation.' Yes, this infatuation happens. It truly does happen because God allows it.

I have experienced it on occasion. Once, it happened to me as I entered the Family Court. I am a lawyer, but this time I wasn't there as an attorney but as one of the litigants. It was the hearing regarding the custody of my son. I was so nervous, filled with anxiety and worry. How wrong we are to be preoccupied with the prefix 'pre.' What little trust in God, right? The worst scenarios played in my mind; my hands were sweating, and my heart pounded so hard it felt like I had just finished a marathon. I wanted to control everything. I reviewed the facts, the dates, opened and closed the folders of documents. I needed to have 'everything under control.' We entered the trial, I took my seat, and I simply said inwardly, 'Holy Spirit, come!'

It is difficult to describe what happened next. There are no words to explain my state of peace. It was as if all the anxiety I had suddenly ended, and a calmness invaded me, carried me effortlessly, enveloped me in a kind of ethereal and pacifying cloud.

All that control I wanted was actually the chain that prevented me from being free, a blindfold that blinded me.

I felt a harmonious peace and an indescribable feeling of love and also a sense of absolute freedom. I had the freedom of God's children. He enveloped me, embraced me, and gave me His peace. I realized that the closer we are to God, the freer we are. Difficult to understand? I don't say it! It's in the Bible, 2 Corinthians 3:17 'for the Lord is the Spirit and where the Spirit of the Lord is, there is freedom.' The Spirit of God enveloped me, and I fell in love with freedom. A freedom that made me 'depend' only on Him, not on men, nor on documents, nor on the defenses I had prepared... That day, GOD and I were the majority. And the hearing? What hearing? I had forgotten it! Sitting there, everything looked different, and you know what? Everything went well because God does everything wonderfully well. It's His pedagogy, teaching us to trust. You surrender and He gives you abundantly, everything according to your faith.

He wanted me to surrender and trust, to make myself small in His presence. In that moment, He made me great and gave me serenity before those who judged me.

The second gift of God was during a routine afternoon in my car. I was driving and thinking about all the things I do wrong, all the mistakes I make, what I propose to amend and don't correct; my sins, my incipient commitment to my Christian duties.

I felt I should demand more of myself, give more, surrender more! I thought maybe I talk too much and do little. 'How tiny I am!' I said to myself, 'How tiny before God!'

A feeling of sadness and desolation began to invade me... Suddenly (for a few brief seconds), I felt as if God passed by my side and enveloped me. He sheltered me and comforted me with infinite tenderness, in a spiritual embrace. God loved me in those seconds, with airs of eternity. He loved me! Tiny, clumsy, inconsequential, nothing and sinful! What beautiful seconds. A delicate feeling of tenderness took hold of my heart, and even today, I can feel it.

I NEVER experienced anything similar from any human being, not from any, father, husband, son, sister... NEVER.

I understood that God does not ask us for great things, nor necessarily the most difficult. He asks us to love. I understood that there is more love in resting and surrendering to Him, trusting like a child in his father, than in worrying about not doing enough. We simply must love. How much? 'The measure of Love is to Love without measure,' Saint Augustine answered.

~23~

"At the end of the age, this is how it will be: The angels will come and separate the wicked from the righteous, and throw them into the blazing furnace, where there will be weeping and gnashing of teeth." (Matthew 13:49-50)

"I dreamed of a vast field, packed with people piled on top of each other. There were hundreds, thousands of them. They had hollow eyes. They were motionless, not moving.

I felt that something serious had happened to them and asked, 'Who are they?' A voice answered me, 'They are the dead souls, those who live in sin.' Then, pointing at one, it added, 'And there you are.'

The next day, still shaken by this dream, I rushed to confess. Since then, I pray for those who live with their souls dead, that God may grant them the grace of conversion.

~24~

"…if you forgive other people when they sin against you, your heavenly Father will also forgive you." Matthew 6:14

Still can't forgive? Experts in these matters explain to us that forgiveness is very beneficial. It's worth forgiving because...

• It increases self-confidence.
• It helps you renew your life.
• It motivates you with new purposes.
• You forget the past and enjoy the present.
• It frees you from the chains of resentment.
• You fill yourself with compassion
  for the person who hurt you.
• It helps you to be humble.

On the other hand, lack of forgiveness causes in us much:

• Anxiety.
• Bitterness.
• Depression.
• Stress.
• Low self-esteem.
• Bad temper.
• Hostility.

~25~

Life is full of paths. I chose the path of God. Sometimes I slip and fall to the side, straying from the path. Then God sends someone who helps me continue. You encounter so many people on this path. Excitedly, they speak to you about God and share their experiences. They have chosen God. They live fully in grace. They enjoy spending time in silence and having moments of intimacy with the good God. Prayer is part of their lives. They reflect on their daily experiences with God. Those little miracles they live every day. They feel, touch, and discover God's presence among them. Their greatest joy is to do the Father's will. To accept with pleasure whatever God sends them. There are so many of them. I find them walking near me. Excitedly, we share our experiences, almost all of them about God's love and tenderness.

I remember a friend who would get emotional to tears every time he mentioned God and told us his adventures. Once he said to us, "The day I die, throw a big party." I mentioned this at work and a young woman asked me, "Why? Is he having such a hard time?" "On the contrary," I said, "the party is because he longs to be with God." Would you like to leave the path you are on and start this journey? It's very simple. We already know where to find it. It's beside you, within you. It's Jesus. "I am the Way, the Truth, and the Life." (Jn 14:6)

~26~

A few years ago, a young woman came to my office to inform me that she was leaving the company. I felt curious and asked her:

— Has someone treated you badly?

— No. Everyone has been very kind to me.

— Is there something you dislike about the job?

— On the contrary, I love it.

— Then why are you leaving? —I asked her— You have a future, stability...

— I am going to Venezuela to work with the Focolare Movement. I could hardly believe it.

— Who are you going with?

— Alone.

It was more than my common sense could grasp. She didn't seem worried. She had such happiness, so much joy within herself... It simply couldn't be! I said goodbye to her, still surprised by this boldness, this risk she was willing to take.

My soul had already been deeply moved. I left for lunch at noon, but I couldn't eat a thing. I drove around in my car to think. It was incredible! How could she? Where did she find the courage? She never knew, but I couldn't help my eyes welling up, even now as I remember it. A great restlessness consumed me.

I told myself, "And you? Coward, what are you doing with your life? Why don't you dare? What are you waiting for? Haven't you heard that He is also calling you?" For Jesus, it's enough to pass by and say, "Follow me." And many go after Him, ecstatic with joy. Without asking, "What do you want from me? Or where will you send me?" They simply follow Him. While others, more cautious, won't step forward without seeing where they will tread. We're not so daring, or maybe we don't love so much... It consoles me to think that He knows what we are made of. He knows our thoughts and sees into the deepest parts of our hearts. "Follow me... Do you want to follow Him? Leave the refuge where we hide. Take risks... Forget about what they'll say, or what they'll think of me. Follow Him openly, against the world if necessary. Let everyone know: 'We belong to Christ.'

A friend did it, took the risk. Sometimes I meet him and he's always happy. I'm amazed at his steadfastness. He confessed to me excitedly: "In my heart there is a seal. And that seal says: JESUS."

This is what happens to those who know Jesus. They have within them that burning fire imprisoned in their bones, and even if they tried to extinguish it, they never could.

~27~

In grace, miracles happen. That's why the saints of the Church were so blessed. In grace, heaven and earth seem to unite, to be one. And you can't distinguish between the eternal and the temporal, because you live in the presence of God. In those moments, God takes great pleasure in His beloved children and gives abundantly whether they ask or not, whether they need or not. He delights in spoiling His own. Sometimes God asks things of us, in such subtle ways that we hardly notice; other times, He speaks to our hearts. We must learn to recognize this voice amidst the noise of the world. When God determines something, you won't find a place to hide. His all-encompassing love will reach you. And you'll say, like St. Augustine, "Late have I loved you."

Something curious happened to me at Mass today. I had just been to confession and sat in one of the central pews. A young man was next to me. I glanced at the confession line, where there were few people, and thought, "He should confess." But I did nothing. After a while, I felt that inner voice urging me: "Tell him to go to confession." "Who am I?" I said to myself. And again, that sweet voice: "Speak to him, tell him to confess." And stubbornly, "How can I tell him to go confess? I can't meddle in his life. I won't do it."

Within a second, the young man stood up, looked at me, and walked towards the confessional, where he confessed. I reflected on what had happened. It was as if God had said to me, "I won't let him be lost. If you don't do it, I will." I knew the young man. After Mass, I approached him and told him what had happened. He looked at me in surprise and said, "I had to confess."

With life so complicated and many difficulties to face, I had forgotten the letter of St. Paul to the Corinthians: "Though I speak with the tongues of men and of angels, but have not love, I have become sounding brass or a clanging cymbal. "God, who is Love, gives meaning to everything. The answer to our concerns will always be the same: "We must love. That's why we are in this world." It was like St. Alberto Hurtado used to say: "Man is in the world because someone loved him: God. Man is in the world to love and to be loved." I was standing amidst the Eucharist, immersed in these thoughts, and suddenly I saw everything so clearly. It had always been there, like an open book, ready to be read by all. The great knowledge I sought, the horizon waiting to be discovered, was no longer the highest mountain or the deepest ocean. What remains for us to attain is the greatest Treasure, the only perfect one: the heart of God. The reward upon opening that infinite heart will be His presence, His mercy, His immense love, perfect knowledge. And the key to open it is love. Time around me had stopped, and marveling, I pondered these things. Something so simple that I had never seen before. In God, everything is simplicity. He loves you and seeks your love. It cannot be simpler than that.

~29~

Today as I see Jesus nailed to the cross, I repent of all the wrong I have done. He suffered for me. And for you. I look into His eyes and say tenderly:

"Your job, Jesus, is to forgive us. Ours is to love you."

~30~

This year began amazingly. I repeated to God many times: "Lord... make me an instrument of your peace." And He immersed me in a conflict I never expected. God takes our words very seriously.

How could I be an instrument of His peace? I needed to possess it, in order to bring it to others. And I found it one morning in prayer, in a small oratory. I went to visit Jesus in the Tabernacle. I stayed with Him and suddenly experienced this supernatural, pure, unimaginable peace that transcended time and overflowed within me. I heard these sweet words:

"Peace I leave with you; my peace I give you. I do not give to you as the world gives. Do not let your hearts be troubled and do not be afraid." (John 14:27)

I left deeply impacted, transformed, knowing that something significant had happened. Then I did what was within my reach, what I believed and thought I should do, but nothing happened to improve the lives of many around me. My means were not enough. I learned that the unreachable, the unexpected, the truly important, He accomplishes it.

We are merely an imperfect reflection of that immense Love that can do all things. And yet, He asks us to love. I wasted much time searching in the wrong places. His Love was the answer, it always was.

I learned to be patient, to wait, and to trust. I learned that humility pleases God. That we must be patient and trust in Him. That everything happens in God's time. And everything happens for a reason.

When the storm disperses, the panorama clears, and you understand that you were never alone. God was always there, in the midst of it all. Waiting for you. Longing for you to seek and recognize His presence. For you to run into His paternal arms, like a child running to their father, to be embraced and comforted.

I often imagine God excited, like a father who watches his child take their first steps... calling them, smiling at them, encouraging each step. I am now aware that God lives with excitement for you, for us. His infinite Love surrounds us and sustains us.

What did I learn?

That we must give our best. That we must trust a little more.

God will NEVER abandon you.

You live in His presence, He is within you, beside you, with you. And He loves you.

~31~

Mother Teresa Quotes

- "If you judge people,
you have no time to love them."

- "Peace begins with a smile."

~32~

THOUGHTS

- This is the hardest part: "Living the Gospel". Interestingly, living it is what brings the most joy.
- Just thinking of God in the mornings brings a happiness that grows throughout the day.
- You can't imagine what a wonderful day I've had. Starting the day with God means ending it with Him.
- Remember: prayer is the language of God.
- As you begin to pray, the world starts to brighten. Suddenly, joy returns to your heart.
- Prayer is essential for happiness.
- Little sheep of God: "Do not be afraid."
- The meaning of life is found in the Cross.
- You are weak because you are not a person of prayer. Prayer strengthens your soul.
- Do you not understand that God loves you despite everything? There are no barriers that can prevent God from loving you. He surpasses everything.
- The search for God lifts us above our fears, our flaws, our desires, our sins...
- Have you felt a wave of tenderness? It's Jesus passing by. He has been near you. You have tasted a piece of heaven. And perhaps you didn't realize it because you were not paying attention.

~33~

Someone said, "Living Host," and I thought: "That's true. The Sacramental host is alive. It's Jesus."

~34~

A priest told me that Saint Philip Neri used to say to Jesus, "Lord, do not neglect Philip." I loved the story. Since that day, I have taken that beautiful prayer for myself and now use it as a short prayer, saying, "Lord, do not neglect Claudio." I also use it for others: "Lord, do not neglect ......" knowing that Jesus will listen to me and to you.

He always listens to us. He is my best friend, since childhood. My great friend. Since I shared this story, many readers write to me, "Claudio, I have taken that beautiful prayer for myself."

~35~

How sad it is to know that Jesus is in the Tabernacle and not to visit Him!

~36~

Offer everything to God. He will take care of you. The secret lies in trusting, surrendering into His loving hands, and offering Him the things we do not like.

~37~

God is good. He knows our thoughts and loves us as we are. It's up to us to respond generously, without fear, knowing that we are called to holiness.

~38~

When you forgive, you will be free. This is what freedom consists of: forgiving. Then you will be happy, your heart will be ready to seek God, and you will lack nothing

~39~

THOUGHTS

- I am like a child in the hands of God. To Him, I have no age. He sees my heart, knows my intentions. And when I fall, He lifts me up, encourages me, urges me to continue, to seek Him more. My Good Jesus. And before Him, I can be who I always wanted to be: more pure, freer, tenderer, filled with more dreams and hopes.
- You are amazed by God's goodness. You begin to taste the sweetness of heaven.
- Do not be discouraged. God tests those He loves.
- Trust in God. That step that seems so small, yet it is everything. The step of complete trust is what makes some good and other saints. They are like an old buoy that refuses to disappear. No matter how much we try to sink it, we will always hear its bell. That's why our greatest treasure is purity of heart.

~40~

With you...

No matter how much we try to hide them, no matter how many years pass, sins always come to light and are visible to God.

~41~

Today I was able to think: "Truly, time does not exist for God. He is timeless." Perhaps in those sweet moments, we are immersing ourselves in the presence of God, in a time that does not exist, in His eternal heaven, in His Love that always prevails. That's why we have that strange sensation that time stops. Because we immerse ourselves in His presence. We breathe in God. We live in God. We feel it, aware that He is within us. As St. Paul said: "In him we live and move and have our being" (Acts 17).

You lead a routine life. Work. Studies. Family. And suddenly, unexpectedly, it happens. God passes by, makes Himself present, and calls you. Your whole life is overturned. It's a moment when it seems like heaven and earth unite. You have the impression that there is no present, only eternity, and it seems that it's not you who dominates the moment, but God. You feel within yourself the immense love of God, which fills your heart, overwhelms you, overflows. And it's so much that you cannot contain it.

You find yourself in a fraction of time that has stopped. It's like the antechamber of heaven. God gives you a taste, bits of heaven. You feel in Paradise. You are deeply immersed in the sea of God, where everything is joy and peace. There are no human words to describe this experience. There is no mountain, forest, or river that compares to what you see. Everything is new, different, beautiful. His presence encompasses everything.

In that moment, you desire to love everyone, to embrace everyonc you meet. You would like to take a megaphone, stand on a corner, and shout to everyone: "God exists. He is alive. He loves you." You want to awaken them from their indifference, let them know that we are important to God. Every sin, no matter how small, pains you. What you once desired loses its value. Suddenly, silence and prayer attract you. And you seek to spend more time alone with God. You and God. In those moments, words are unnecessary. Your heart longs for His presence. His Love is all that matters. A supernatural joy overwhelms you. You now know that you are not alone, that you never were, that God loves you above all things, despite everything... and yearns for your love.

At that moment, the words of St. Teresa make sense: "God alone suffices." You understand that you need nothing more. It's as if you wake up from a long dream. You see everything clearly. You understand that you searched in the wrong places. It's not money or fame, or friends, or life itself. Only one thing is important: "To love." To love everyone, even those who do not love you, those who hurt you, those who love you. To love them in a true love that transcends, embraces, and transforms. A love that is not yours, but God's.

~42~

Daughter of God do not be afraid.
He cares for you. He walks with you.
He embraces you.
Everything will be alright.

~43~

Today I repeat it to you. Be brave. Do not be afraid. God is with you, beside you, within you.

~44~

Did you know?
God becomes happy
when we trust in Him.

~45~

"Do not despise, my son, the instruction of Yahweh, and do not be weary of his reproof, for Yahweh reproves those he loves, as a father the son in whom he delights."

Proverbs 3:11-12

Do not be discouraged.
God tests those he loves.

~46~

"The secret of wisdom, of a woman of faith, is to love God. For God delights in those who love him.

The secret is to surrender oneself into the arms of God. Whoever surrenders to God lacks nothing. The secret is to give, for whoever gives receives."

~47~

Seeking wisdom? You must know this,
it comes from the Bible.

"Wisdom will not enter a deceitful soul,
nor dwell in a body enslaved by sin."

Wisdom 1:4

~48~

Mother Teresa Quotes

"Yesterday is gone.
Tomorrow has not yet come.
We have only today.
Let us begin."

. "If you find happiness, people may be jealous. Be happy anyway."

"A life not lived for others is not a life."

"I prefer you to make mistakes in kindness than work miracles in unkindness."

"Love is a fruit in season at all times and within reach of every hand."

~49~

THOUGHTS

- How good it is to be able to offer something to Jesus, even if it's just a smile made in His name, or the fever that consumes us.
- What sublime feelings the priest must have at the moment of consecration.
- The true follower is tested in humility and obedience.
- Fill your day with small acts of love for Jesus.
- Jesus, you are the comfort of souls. You always answer our prayers.
- How many souls are waiting for our prayers and do not receive them because we are busy with other things.
- You climb another step towards heaven. How much each step costs!
- What joy to know that the good God never abandons us!
- Trust in God, your Father.

~50~

Since I rediscovered God, I never tire of seeking Him. It's a supernatural feeling, a longing for God that draws us towards His Love. I'm sitting in a rocking chair as I write to you. I look around and gratefully think of all the beautiful things God has given us. Of all the graces with which He adorns our lives. Yours and mine because we are siblings.

This experience is recognizing that we have lived thirsty, walking in a desert, exhausted, without strength, when next to us we have an inexhaustible source of joy, available to whoever wants to take from it. We are surrounded by an endless oasis, with juicy dates, huge palm trees that provide refreshing shade. There are rivers of crystal-clear water to quench our thirst. You enter the oasis and never want to leave it again. You know that outside the only thing you will find is suffocating heat, useless exhaustion, a meaningless life. It's useless to struggle alone against difficulties. We have God as an ally to guide us. I reflect on the things of God trying to understand them. When you discover God's presence in your life, everything else loses value to you. You incessantly seek solitary places to be with Him. Every church then becomes a refuge to be in His presence, an environment that brings us serenity, with an atmosphere that invites prayer.

~51~

I love visiting silent chapels that invite prayer. What has always impressed me about chapels is the Tabernacle. Knowing that Jesus dwells there, hidden, waiting, silent. Since I was a child, He was my neighbor in the city of Colon. We lived on Ninth Street, across from the Servants of Mary. They had a beautiful chapel. His presence was what impressed me the most. There was God. Many times, alone. Waiting. I used to cross the street to visit Him. I loved spending those unforgettable moments with Him. In my child's heart, I imagined Him alone, in need of a friend. And I wanted to be His friend.

I used to work at a company where people often visited me and for some reason told me about the problems they were facing. I remember taking a piece of paper, writing a few words, and handing them this "spiritual prescription," like a pharmacist would. I folded the piece of paper and said, "Open it at home." They often returned to thank me for the advice. The change was surprising. Almost all of them said the same thing: "Visit Jesus in the Tabernacle. He has the answers." With these prescriptions, I ended up writing a book.

One of the most impressive anecdotes was about my friend José. He had lost his job and was restless. He had a family, a mortgage. When he told me about it, I remember saying, "You are in this situation because you want to be."

He looked at me surprised. "Have you visited Jesus yet? Go and tell Him everything. Tell Him that you need this job not for yourself but to support your family." The next day, my friend returned. This time with a different look. He could hardly contain himself. "You won't believe it," he said. "I did what you suggested. When I got home, the moment I opened the door, the phone started ringing. They were calling to offer me a job! Can you believe it?"

From the Tabernacle, Jesus sees you and listens to you. He fills you with His grace and His Love. I have experienced it. It's not something I read in a book or was told. That's why I share it with you. What you seek, what keeps your heart restless, your answers... you can find it all in the Tabernacle.

"Who can find* a woman of worth?
Far beyond jewels is her value."
Proverbs 31, 10.

~52~

Have you noticed? We are very comfortable in our jobs, in our everyday situations, not progressing, and suddenly something happens that changes everything. And even though it may not seem like it, it's for our own good. God always sets us "on the path".

~53~

Many years ago, I heard a young girl say that she "was worth nothing." She knew she was a child of God and described herself with the worst adjectives imaginable.

She looked at me again and asked, "And you, what do you think?"

For some reason, I replied, "Me?... Well, I think little. I live trying to trust despite my humanity and the doubts that arise from time to time. But I also live with certainties... The certainty of knowing that there is an Almighty God for whom nothing is impossible. A God who created us all and, to our joy, is my Father, your Father, our Father."

I looked at her, smiled, and continued:

"I don't know who told you that you are worth little, but what I do know is that person was completely wrong. You are worth a lot, too much, in the eyes of God. When you doubt whether you are valuable or not, look at a cross. Then you will understand."

~54~

Do you sometimes feel a wave of tenderness? It's God passing by. And He touches hearts. He transforms them. He fills them with His Love.

~55~

I have always felt grateful because my parents enrolled me in a Catholic school in the city of Colon. It was the Pauline College of San José. Sweet Franciscan nuns taught the classes. Some still remember them with joy and speak to me about them: Sister María Ávila, Sister Louitgarda, Sister Fermina. On those sunny mornings, they spoke to us about God, the love of Jesus, the Virgin Mary, Saint Joseph, and told us stories about our Guardian Angel, ending with what was, for me, a delightful dessert: "the life of Saint Francis of Assisi."

I remember a song that said, "We are the pilgrims going towards heaven..." I thought about that wonderful place the nuns spoke to us about. I imagined myself playing among the clouds as if they were an amusement park. I amused myself by eating sugary clouds with fruit syrup and milkshake. Traveling at the speed of thought among the stars and planets. Now that I am older, I realize that Heaven is much better than I imagined. There, only happiness, purity, simplicity, innocence, and Love exist. Heaven is being with God. That is why Saint Teresa of Jesus said, "Where God is, there is Heaven."

When you live in the presence of God, with a pure soul, you begin to taste small pieces of Heaven. You live, as a priest friend would say, in "the antechamber of Heaven."

~56~

With you...

It's not about how much money you have. Wealth won't make you happy. If you don't have God, nothing will fill your soul with joy. I have read many biographies, books that narrate the lives of saints. All of them, without exception, had these things in common:

1. They prayed fervently.
2. They found happiness in the loving presence of God.
3. They never regretted spending their lives on something greater than themselves.
4. They trusted in God.
5. They knew they were beloved children of God.
6. They were devoted to the Virgin Mary and Saint Joseph.
7. They didn't need to accumulate possessions. Their treasures were in heaven. God always provided for their needs.
8. They discovered that humility pleases God greatly and they strove to obtain that grace.
9. They were citizens of heaven.
10. They found Jesus in the poor.
11. They lived by Divine Providence.

~57~

God expects great things from you. And what matters most to Him and excites Him the most, is your love. He wants you to love greatly and Him, to love Him more.

~58~

Years teach you the value of prayer and humility. How difficult both are for us... To pray and to be humble. To pray to be with God. To spend moments of intimacy in His loving presence. And humility to be able to approach Him.

Saint Augustine said: "If you want to be holy, be humble. If you want to be very holy, be very humble; if you want to be even more holy, be even more humble." This is the hallmark that distinguishes the children of God when they have attained grace and a degree of holiness. You recognize them by their humility and a life of prayer.

How is it going for you? As for me... I have not yet attained those degrees of humility. I am still struggling against the Claudio that I am, looking towards the Claudio that I want to be. I am like those who travel to Santiago de Compostela: "on the way."

~59~

Sometimes we must go through a difficult situation in order to understand. It's something that doesn't always make sense. We've been taught that everything that happens to us is for our own good. If you look around, it might seem a bit illogical. That's the problem. Our temporal logic cannot encompass God's timeless thinking. There's much I don't understand, and I often pray, "Lord, I want to understand." And in response, I find myself in a situation I don't desire. That's God's pedagogy. To strengthen a bush, it must be fertilized, watered, and pruned. That's the painful part, when God prunes us. Sometimes I get tired, find it hard to understand, and I dedicate myself to trusting. It seems that everything is given to us little by little. Once I asked Him, "Why don't you give us everything at once?"

That night I had a dream. I was before Him. I stared at Him. He had a sack of oranges, opened it, and threw all the oranges at me. I caught 6 or 7; the rest rolled on the ground. Then He smiled gently, and this dialogue began: "How many did you catch?" I looked at Him ashamed. "A few," I replied. And I apologized: "I only have two hands, Lord. I can't handle so many at once." He looked at me compassionately and added: "With my grace it's the same. I give it little by little so it's not wasted and can be used well.

~60~

Last night something unexpected happened. I was at the Easter Resurrection Mass with my wife, Vida, and I started to ponder: "Lord, you have commanded us to love one another." I looked around at the people attending Mass and said to Him, "But how can I love those I don't know? Where do I find that love that I don't have? I don't know these people, I don't know their stories, and they don't know me. The only thing we have in common is our faith and the fact that you have called us here."

I remembered some words from Chiara Lubich, the founder of the Focolare Movement, about how love should be: "We must love first. Love everyone. Love, even if we are not loved in return." I felt like leaving, but I decided to stay. It's not natural for me to want to leave when I'm at Mass. At that moment, I didn't know that this temptation was trying to deprive me of a grace. I stayed and participated in Mass with Vida. I felt full of concerns and decided to pray, asking God to show me His ways, to tell me how to do things, to explain to me how to love. And I asked for His Holy Spirit. I knew that God, in His infinite goodness, is pleased when His children ask Him as children do and He grants their requests with innocence and purity of heart. I approached to receive communion, and as I was returning to my seat, something happened that overwhelmed me and almost paralyzed me where I stood. I saw a radiant light covering all of us inside the church. It was a marvelous sight. A light that did not hurt my eyes and made me feel special, different, loved. In that moment, I began to experience a love so great, immense, within me, like a dam breaking and its waters flooding the channel. It was a rushing river that engulfed me and carried me along with it. And its waters were formed by the purest love you can imagine. A love untouched by selfishness or pride. An almost childlike, naive, simple love that gives itself without reservation, without asking for anything in return. And suddenly, unexpectedly, I began to love. I didn't have to do anything special. I had immersed myself in the sea of God, in His love, and it was that love that allowed me to love. I loved with His love. I couldn't believe what was happening to me. I stood up and began to walk through the church, looking at everyone. "I can love them!" I exclaimed in surprise. I took out a piece of paper and wrote so as never to forget that moment: "Suddenly, I have loved them. I was capable of embracing each one." I saw a friend, approached the pew where he was sitting, embraced him, and said, "I embrace the Jesus who lives in you." I was deeply moved. I realized, that was the answer!! Our love will always be insufficient. How can we love with a love far from pure and noble? That's impossible. I fully understood Jesus' parable when He related us to the vine and said, "Apart from me you can do nothing." When I received communion, Jesus granted me the grace to experience a tiny portion of His love, as small as I was capable of receiving it at that moment. It was an overflowing love, I couldn't contain it.

It moved me to love. It became a necessity: to love them all.

~61~

This morning, feeling calmer, I sat down to reflect on yesterday's wonderful experience during Mass, and I said to myself in admiration:

"What must Jesus' love be like in its fullness? Such a great, immense love that moved Him to die for us and to remain in every Tabernacle around the world, motionless, without moving, patiently waiting for someone to visit Him."

Once I asked Him: "What do you do all day in the Tabernacle? I can move around, walk through the house, go out for a walk, read a book, talk with my family. What about you?"

It seemed to me He responded: "Love, Claudio. Love them all... From the Tabernacle, I watch over them and love them."

~62~

An Australian nurse, Bronnie Ware, dedicated many years working in the palliative care section of a hospital, caring for dying patients and spending endless hours talking with them, listening to them, and encouraging them. From her experiences, she wrote a book titled "The Top Five Regrets of the Dying." In it, she recounted that at the end of their lives, the biggest regret, the most frequent one was:"I wish I had the courage to live a life true to myself, not the life others expected of me."

We should consider what God expects of us and not what we imagine others think or expect of us. We must discover what God asks of us, and for that, you must read the Bible. He expects you to be merciful, just, forgiving, and to help everyone you can whenever you can.

The thought "what will people think of me" has ruined many lives, dreams, and promising futures. Do you think it's worth spending your life on something so unproductive that will ultimately not make you happy? Maybe you see it as necessary now, but believe me, it's not worth it; you're wasting your valuable time and harming yourself. You don't deserve it; you're not just anything or a random fruit. You were created out of love, you live by love, and God looks at you with infinite, unique love of his own.

~63~

Sometimes I think it's incomprehensible for us to be loved so much despite who we are and what we do, but God, who is love, cannot help but love and expect more from you. Believe me... you are called to transcend, to be happy, and to bear fruits of eternity. In God's hands, everything will be alright.

"Lord, help me live the wonderful life you have prepared for me."

Do you know what else makes us live restless, fearful lives? Sin, a guilty conscience. The Bible, in Genesis 3, tells us what happened after Eve and Adam disobeyed God's command. Pay attention: "Then the man and his wife heard the sound of the Lord God as he was walking in the garden in the cool of the day, and they hid from the Lord God among the trees of the garden. But the Lord God called to the man, 'Where are you?' He answered, 'I heard you in the garden, and I was afraid because I was naked; so I hid.'"

~64~

I assure you, nothing gives as much peace as having a pure soul, in a state of grace.

"For it is by grace you have been saved through faith, and this is not from yourselves, it is the gift of God." Ephesians 2:8

~65~

"Dear friends, let us love one another, for love comes from God. Everyone who loves has been born of God and knows God." 1 John 4:7

I don't know you. I imagine you're going through a dark moment because you've been hurt and can't stop hating or seeking revenge. I don't know what thoughts you have, or why; perhaps your mind is playing tricks on you and making you feel it's time for payback for the harm done to you. I don't know. But I do know that God has a special preference for you. He loves you. He wants you to be happy. He asks you to be holy, to forgive, to love, to be merciful to everyone.

In a way that I don't fully understand, God wants to console you, to let you know He is with you, that there is no need to fear, that you can forgive, that you have that capacity, and that everything will be alright. I apologize if I'm writing these things, but it's imperative that you know:

"God loves you. You are important to Him."

~66~

"Live praying and supplicating. Pray at all times as the Spirit inspires you. Watch together and persevere in your prayers without ever becoming discouraged, interceding for all the saints, your brothers." Ephesians 6

There is a wonderful quality that distinguishes those who long to see their dreams realized: "Persistence." I suppose it's a quality that distinguishes those who love their craft. You don't give up along the way. You don't let obstacles stop you. If you fall, you get back up again. That's what you must do to succeed... especially in faith. You must never give up in the face of adversity.

Give deeper meaning to what you do. Make every minute count.

- Pray.
- Love.
- Forgive.
- Live joyfully in your faith.
- Set an example with your life.
- And never give up.

~67~

I have learned that the merit lies not in doing, but in trusting. God wants us to trust in Him, to love Him.

~68~

"God, who created you without you, will not save you without you." Saint Augustine

Are you living indulging in a sin? Then you are not truly living. You carry a dead soul like an empty sack. Don't lose a wonderful eternity for a fleeting pleasure.

Saint Josemaria Escriva once remarked on the beauty of purity: "One cannot lead a clean life without divine assistance. God wants our humility, He wants us to ask for His help, through our mother and His Mother."

Do not hesitate to turn to the Virgin; ask for her maternal help, and she will never deny it to you.

~69~

I don't remember if I ever told you. The best things have happened to me in a church. In one of them, I saw the woman who is now my wife. Curiously, during Mass, I get the best ideas. That's why I always carry paper and a pencil with me. Sometimes I run out of paper and use the Catholic weekly to write on its margins. There are so many ideas that I say to Jesus, "Slow down, I can't write that fast."

I remember an occasion when I spent months trying to understand why some people seem to receive everything from God while others seem to receive very little or nothing at all. There must be a reason, but I couldn't find it.

I had spoken with some priests, and they all told me the same thing: "You must find the answer." But I felt further from it each time. During Mass, right at the moment of the Offertory, suddenly everything around me lit up. It felt as if heavy blinders fell from my eyes, and I could see and understand.

It was one of the most emotional moments of my life. I could hardly believe it. The answer was right in front of me. For the first time, I wanted Mass to end quickly so I could go home and write. I left as soon as I could and sat down to write. I titled the book:

"The Great Secret" How to obtain what you ask of God.

I finished it in a short time. It's the book that took me the longest to understand, the one I wrote the fastest, and the one with the most editions.

Sometimes I wonder, why during Mass? Why not in a park or in my living room? I've always been curious about this detail. And today, a priest in his homily helped me understand how extraordinary Mass is. Its infinite value, why they call it "the antechamber of heaven."

In each Mass, you leave the earthly, temporal dimension and enter "the Trinitarian dimension, the dimension of eternal life." It's like being with God in heaven. During the Eucharist, you participate in "the perfect prayer," the one most pleasing to God, and you enter into the presence of the Holy Trinity.

It's comforting to know that those who go to Mass every day to be with the Lord, to praise Him, and to receive Him into their souls, have not been mistaken.

~70~

"Make me know your ways, O Lord; teach me your paths. Guide me in your truth and teach me, for you are God my Savior, and my hope is in you all day long." Psalm 25:4-5

We all have the ability to change and renew our lives. It depends on us to do so. I have seen it so many times—people who, from one day to the next, decide for God and their lives take on meaning. Most have made resolutions to change, to do things differently, and it has gone well for them. When I made the decision to live for God, I never imagined the great adventures I was about to experience. Every day has been a wonderful encounter with God. Since that morning when I stepped out of the car to reflect and offer Him what remained of my life, the good Lord has not stopped filling me with gifts and graces.

At first, I knew very little. Everything seemed new and different to me. I thought that the saints, having walked the right path, would have the answers. So, I began to read their biographies. I was not mistaken. They had much to teach me. I recommend you read them; you can find them at your favorite Catholic bookstore. They will change your life.

~71~

It's wonderful, every day I encounter people like myself, weak, with flaws, but who wanted to overcome themselves and find God. They managed to find Him thanks to:

- Prayer.
- Daily communion.
- Frequent confession.
- Reading the Bible.
- Reading Catholic books on spirituality.
- Living a sacramental life.
- Surrendering themselves.
- Accepting the Divine Will.
- Trusting in God.
- Their unshakable faith.
- Their desire for perfection.
- Their longing to serve and love others.
- The good resolutions they made.
- The joy of living.

Are you willing to give it a try?

~72~

One day I set out to seek God. Along this journey, I encountered Saint Francis de Sales. You have no idea how much I have admired him. Don Bosco took his name for the congregation he was forming and called it the "Salesians." Saint Francis de Sales wrote these resolutions in memory of his First Communion and strove throughout his life to fulfill them. It is worth imitating him.

1. Every morning and every night, I will pray some prayers.
2. Whenever I pass in front of a Church, I will enter to visit Jesus in the Blessed Sacrament, unless there is a serious reason that prevents me from doing so.
3. Always and whenever possible, I will help the poorest and most needy people.
4. I will read good books, especially Lives of Saints.

I would like to add to you some resolutions that have personally helped me in my search for Truth. They have aided me in getting up every time I fall.

1. I will endeavor to attend Mass every day. I will participate devoutly and receive Holy Communion.

2. I will confess frequently, even if they are only venial sins.
3. I will carry with me a medal or the Scapular of the Virgin, and every night before sleeping, I will say my prayers and give it a kiss, grateful for the protection provided by our Heavenly Mother.
4. Before sleeping, I will remember to thank my Guardian Angel for his favors.
5. I will always keep in mind the Holy Souls in Purgatory in my prayers.
6. I will attentively listen to the priests' homilies and follow their advice.
7. I will strive to see Christ in the poor and needy, offering a word of encouragement or advice.
8. I will ask God for wisdom to understand His plans and love to love others with a pure and clean love.

~73~

To God, it pleases Him to know that we love Him. Don't you know Psalm 53? It says:

"God looks down from heaven on all mankind to see if there are any who understand, any who seek God." We seek God, and God seeks us.

~74~

To forgive gives you the opportunity of a new life.

~75~

I have often asked myself this question. And I have heard many others asking the same. I used to say: "Lord, where are you?" And it seemed to me that He responded: "Here beside you, in you... where I have always been."

~76~

"What good is it for someone to gain the whole world, and yet lose or forfeit their very self?" Luke 9:25

We get caught up in so many worldly activities. If they do not lead us to heaven, what purpose do they serve?

~77~

As Catholics, it is good to remember these truths:

1. The devil exists and is cruel, cunning, he hates us.
2. Hell exists.
3. Purgatory exists.
4. Heaven exists.
5. We are called to be holy.
6. We can help with our prayers.

~78~

Today I read these words from Chiara Lubich, the founder of the Focolare Catholic Movement. I found them extraordinary, so I'm sharing them with you:

"As Christians, we are called to contribute to 'that all may be one,' so let us first renew our faith that every human being is called to unity, because God loves everyone.

And let's not make excuses: 'That person will never understand'; or 'this one is too young to comprehend'; or 'this is my relative, I know them well, they are attached to earthly things'; 'that person belongs to another faith'; 'this one is too old to change.'

No: let go of all these judgments. God loves everyone, waits for everyone."

~79~

Today I saw a garden and thought, "If we plant tomato seeds, tomatoes grow; if we plant cucumber seeds, cucumbers grow. What if we plant seeds of love in the heart of humanity? Everything would be better."

~80~

12:00 p.m. The church bells have just rung at the church near my house. They call to the Angelus prayer. A wonderful devotion. Put it into practice. Let's honor the Virgin Mary. The custom among the faithful is to pray it at noon.

The angel of the Lord declared unto Mary. And she conceived by the Holy Spirit.
Hail Mary...

Behold the handmaid of the Lord. Be it done unto me according to your word.
Hail Mary...

And the Word was made flesh. And dwelt among us.
Hail Mary...

Pray for us, O Holy Mother of God, that we may be made worthy of the promises of Christ.

Let us pray.

Pour forth, we beseech you, O Lord, your grace into our hearts, that we, to whom the incarnation of Christ your Son was made known by the message of an angel, may by his passion and cross be brought to the glory of his resurrection. Through Christ our Lord. Amen.

~81~

I know it may not be easy what you're going through, but don't worry, this too shall pass. You'll be fine. I leave you with these two Bible verses, perhaps among the most read in the Bible. They are in Philippians 4:6-7 and Philippians 4:13.

"Do not be anxious about anything, but in every situation, by prayer and petition, with thanksgiving, present your requests to God. And the peace of God, which transcends all understanding, will guard your hearts and your minds in Christ Jesus."

"I can do all things through Him
who strengthens me."
Philippians 4:13

~82~

I pray for you. I don't know you,
but I pray for you.

Everything will be fine,
don't worry.

~83~

I know it's not easy what you're going through. But don't worry. Follow the advice of Father Pio. It works wonders.

"Pray, hope, and don't worry. Worry is useless. God is merciful and will hear your prayer..."

~84~

It's not easy, I know. You've been hurt.
And it hurts. You can overcome it.
You are strong.

~85~

"Then Peter came to Jesus and asked, 'Lord, how many times shall I forgive my brother or sister who sins against me? Up to seven times?'" (Matthew 18:21)

Jesus asks you to love. To forgive 70 times 7. Feeling like you can't? Let me tell you what I've learned.

Forgiving is hard when you've been hurt, when you've received unkindness, injustice, and you feel like returning the harm. Believe me, pride and hatred are not good advisers. Stay away from them.

Persist in your trust and prayer. You will try to love, and in doing so, you surrender to God's loving hands, and suddenly one morning, almost without realizing it, you discover that, with God's grace and love, everything becomes possible. Everything becomes simpler. And you are capable of loving and forgiving. Not by your own strength, but by His.

~86~

Do not be afraid.
There is no reason to be.
God is Almighty.
And He is our Father.

~87~

In your difficulties, turn to the Virgin Mary, the mother of Jesus, our Savior. Who protects her child better than a mother?

The Virgin will never abandon you. Always be a faithful child and she will cover you with her protective mantle.

CONSECRATION TO THE VIRGIN

"O my Lady! O my Mother! I offer myself entirely to you; and as proof of my filial affection, I consecrate to you today my eyes, my ears, my tongue, my heart: in a word, all my being. Since I am all yours, O Mother of goodness, guard and defend me as your own possession and property. Amen."

~88~

I understand you. Life is not easy and sometimes it gets more complicated than we can handle. These are the moments when fear paralyzes us. We fill ourselves with anguish. What to do? Recently, a young woman wrote to me facing multiple problems. She asked for a word of encouragement to help her keep going. The simplest and yet the deepest word came to my mind, one that I've seen change hundreds of lives: "Trust. Have faith." I knew from experience that we must trust; it's what God expects from us. Trust, despite everything. Trust, even when we don't understand what's happening to us. Trust, knowing that, no matter how complicated or painful it seems, what happens to us will always be for our good.

It's God's pedagogy. Perhaps He wants to make you more humble, or teach you not to cling to the temporal, or show you His tenderness and strengthen your faith. God's ways are not understood in temporal terms. He is eternal and thinks in terms of eternity. We think in human terms, with our limitations. Therefore, instead of trying to understand why God has allowed it, it is best to simply surrender ourselves into His loving hands and trust. With the simplicity of a child who loves and obeys their Father. With the heart of innocence and purity. Nothing bad can happen to us when we are with God. He created the world, the heavens, the stars. Do you think a small problem will overwhelm Him?

~89~

"In peace I will lie down and sleep, for you alone, Lord, make me dwell in safety."

Psalm 4:9

"Not long ago, I met a humble person. I always see him cheerful, so I dared to ask him what he does. 'When I have a problem,' he replied, 'I kneel down and talk to God. Being in His presence comforts me and I regain peace.'"

~90~

We are more alike than you think. I believe we all share our concerns, dreams, aspirations, and desires. We all seek happiness and understanding, someone to share our joys with.

I don't possess:

- The strength and serenity of Job.
- The confidence and faith of Abraham.
- The obedience of Saint Joseph.
- The prayer life of a monk.
- The kindness of Mother Teresa.

But in my heart, I have a seed ready to sprout. That seed is called "holiness." I search and find, and each time I find, I am filled with more questions. It's curious. Instead of these virtues, I have been filled with questions. I seek God. I long to understand the meaning of life. I question many of the things God allows. I believe He sees my concerns as a virtue because He always answers me. And He does so in the most incredible way you can imagine. Once I asked Him, "Why do I have to face so many obstacles? Why don't you give me abundant blessings?" That same day, I opened a little book of reflections and came across this decisive phrase: "If you had everything, you wouldn't be able to know my Providence." That day, I stopped asking and doubting to devote myself to trust.

~91~

The Holy Bible is full of advice, positive thoughts, optimism, and a path of holiness and purity. We are constantly told, "Do not be afraid." It's a phrase that Jesus often uses, especially when He appears to the apostles.

Life is simple. Do not be afraid. Live it to the fullest. Do not listen to anyone who tells you otherwise. You are a brave, wonderful woman with great values, and God looks upon you with pleasure.

God loves you. He has given you life so that you can do great things with it. Set goals, have purposes. Be happy. Reclaim your life. Do not let yourself be defeated. Cheer up!

~92~

Gratitude. A forgotten word. Today we are going to have a very special day. It will be a day for gratitude, giving thanks to God. With your heart in your hand, give thanks for the way He has guided your life. Because everything, no matter how complicated or unfair it may seem, has a wonderful purpose, an extraordinary reason that you will discover in God's Plan, your Father, with time.

"The Lord is my strength and my shield; my heart trusted in him, and I am helped. Therefore, my heart greatly rejoices, and with my song I will praise him."

Psalm 28:7

~93~

"Jesus, I trust in you.

Against all odds and despite everything.
I trust in you."

~94~

"Do you think no one loves you?
God loves you... from Eternity."

~95~

I often say that if God had another name,
I would call Him "Tenderness."

I am certain that He has been present in every moment
of your life, accompanying you, watching over you,
holding your hand like a little child.

God never abandons you.

~96~

Jeremiah 29:13 "When you search for me, you will find me; if you seek me with all your heart."

Have you ever felt the loving presence of God?

It's like a gentle flutter in the soul. You know it's Him. God passing by. And it leaves you with unimaginable peace. Immense joy. Love overflowing. You're left longing to know Him more and live close to Him.

~97~

John 14:27 "Peace I leave with you; my peace I give you. I do not give to you as the world gives. Do not let your hearts be troubled and do not be afraid."

I remember fondly that friend of mine whom I encountered one day in the Church. — It's been a long time since I've been here — he reflected. He looked around and remarked admirably. — There is a great peace here. — That's why I come, whenever I can — I replied. — It's the peace that only God can give us.

~98~

Isaiah 43:1-3

"Do not fear, for I have redeemed you; I have called you by name; you are mine. When you pass through the waters, I will be with you; and when you pass through the rivers, they will not overwhelm you. When you walk through the fire, you will not be burned; the flames will not set you ablaze. For I am Yahweh your God, the Holy One of Israel, your Savior."

I heard about this young man who spent his entire life seeking God. Suddenly, a deadly illness struck him. He lay wasting away in his hospital bed. Some observed the serenity with which he faced his fate and asked him: — Why? How? Aren't you afraid? — All my life I've longed to see God face to face — he replied. — Should I fear now that this dream will come true?

~99~

When Pope Benedict XVI was Cardinal, he wrote these words that helped me live with more intensity and joy: "Being holy does not mean being superior to others; on the contrary, the saint can be very weak and have many mistakes in his life. Holiness is deep contact with God, becoming friends with God, letting the Other, the Only One who can really make this world good and happy, act."

— Being holy is being a friend of God.

I reflected on this and said to myself, surprised:

— Is it that simple?

It was as if the fog in a forest had lifted. I saw the path so clearly that I was filled with supernatural joy. I felt flooded with peace and trust, as when a dam breaks and its waters flood everything. My soul floated in the midst of that infinite vastness of the Father. My life was a ship that spread its sails waiting for the wind and that He chose when to blow, to sail into the sea. I decided to be a friend of God. Living in Providence. Accept all of His Holy Will. I have never been so happy.

~100~

Somewhere I read that this was perfect joy: surrendering into God's arms, confident, without fear. At my age, it wasn't easy for me, I must admit. I have a beautiful family. Vida, my wife, cares for us diligently. God has entrusted us with 4 children... and despite these wonderful treasures, I am filled with concerns. When everyone was asleep, I would get out of bed, go to the living room, and in the silence of the night, I would ask, "What do you want from me, Lord?" I listened in the silence, another silence, His voice clear and transparent like the purest crystal. A profound silence that is hard to understand. For months, my mind and heart were filled with hundreds of questions and concerns. Has this ever happened to you? You feel so close to the answer, the oasis, the calm, yet you cannot reach it. His Word followed me everywhere: at work, at home, in the car. His immensity overwhelmed me. This Psalm echoed in my mind, making me acknowledge my great weakness, my smallness, and His immense greatness to surrender in His love: "Lord, you have searched me and you know me; you know when I sit and when I rise; you perceive my thoughts from afar. You discern my going out and my lying down; you are familiar with all my ways. Before a word is on my tongue you, Lord, know it completely. You hem me in behind and before, and you lay your hand upon me. Such knowledge is too wonderful for me, too lofty for me to attain. Where can I go from your Spirit? Where can I flee from your presence?"

~101~

"Trust in the Lord with all your heart, and do not rely on your own understanding. In all your ways acknowledge him, and he will make your paths straight."

Proverbs 3:5-6

God does what is best for us. But it's not always what we expect, because it's hard for us to understand. Maybe we're not meant to understand, but to have faith. In the end, I realized that everything boils down to trust, letting go of doubts and trusting. This is true freedom. Letting go of everything and resting in his hands.

~102~

"God is our refuge and strength, an ever-present help in times of trouble. Therefore, we will not fear, even if the earth trembles and the mountains topple into the depths of the sea; even if its waters roar and foam, and the mountains quake with their surging. The Lord Almighty is with us."

Psalm 46

Today, before we begin our daily activities, let us say a brief prayer from the heart, for all of us who need God so much.

Repeat with me:

Lord, you know all things. You know my weaknesses, my little faith. Teach me to trust, to never doubt you. And grant me the grace to console those who come to me in need.

~103~

Do not be discouraged. Everything will turn out well. When we live in the presence of Jesus, and have Him by our side, success is assured.

"As long as you remain in me and my words remain in you, ask whatever you wish, and it will be done for you" (John 15:7).

It's God; is anything impossible for Him?

I've been thinking about prayer for days. How much we need it, and how much I need it too. Have you gotten used to talking to God? Father Angel said in one of his retreats, "Whoever does not pray does not need a devil to tempt him." Those who do not pray live in such spiritual weakness that any whisper from the devil will make them fall. St. John Chrysostom has a thought that clarifies the value of prayer: "Nothing is as valuable as prayer: it makes possible what is impossible, it makes easy what is difficult." Prayer is so important, this intimate and close conversation with our Heavenly Father, that we can never fully measure its impact on earth. I used to think that prayer was God's language. It doesn't matter in which language you pray; He will always understand. Now I think that prayer is placing ourselves in the loving presence of God. I asked some young people I found gathered in a parish, "How can a young woman know what God wants from her?" They responded, "Through prayer." As I was leaving, the most enthusiastic one approached me to say, "And if this young woman thinks she doesn't know how to pray, tell her not to worry. God will hear her anyway."

Chiara Lubich wrote: "We cannot live without breathing, and prayer is the breath of the soul, the expression of our love for God." It's true, I thought, so many souls perish for lack of prayer. They fall into mortal sin so easily.

~105~

God will never disappoint you.

~106~

I have thirsted for God. Just as the psalmist said, "My soul thirsts for you, my flesh faints for you." And I locked myself in a room of the house to be with God. To speak to Him with my heart. So I began this beautiful dialogue, between Him, almighty, and me, a mere mortal. Like Francis of Assisi asked Him: "Who are you? Who am I?" I opened my little book of Psalms and read: "On my bed I remember you; I think of you through the watches of the night." I was lying down and said to Him in surprise: "This is what I do, Lord, I meditate on you, I remember you." Suddenly, I felt an immense and profound love surrounding me and filling me. "It is You," I said, amazed.

I understood, with my great limitation: His majesty, power, how infinite and omnipotent the Father is. He sees everything, and I barely see with my eyes and my heart. He is immense and I am small. He is the Creator and I am His creature. I recognized that His love surpasses all understanding. That for us, He gives everything; and for us, it is His love. I ended these reflections with these verses from Psalm 63:

"Your steadfast love is better than life. My lips will praise you. So I will bless you as long as I live; in your name I will lift up my hands. My soul will be satisfied as with fat and rich food, and my mouth will praise you with joyful lips.

~107~

Nothing compares to the love of God.
Before Him, everything loses its value.
It's like they used to say
Saint Teresa of Avila:

Let nothing disturb you,
let nothing frighten you,
all things are passing away:
God never changes.
Patience obtains all things.
Whoever has God lacks nothing;
God alone suffices.

~108~

"For God so loved the world that he gave his one and only Son, that whoever believes in him shall not perish but have eternal life." John 3:16

Did you know that Saint Francis loved God so much that he was terrified at the mere thought of offending Him? He wept through the forests of Assisi crying out, "Love is not loved! Love is not loved!" He even had a companion to confess immediately any wrong thought, anything that might offend the tender heart of our God.

~109~

What should I do?

Reconcile with God. Start taking care of your soul and the state of grace, like a treasure given to you for happiness. A saint once said:

"You have only one soul.
If you lose it, what will you do?"

Strive to do what God asks of you: pray, forgive, love, live in His loving presence. Your good deeds will be engraved in God's heart.

There is still time. I am sure you can achieve it. We have the time of grace and mercy that God grants to us all.

Do not close your heart to the call of the Eternal Father. Aspire to the most beautiful: holiness. Live the extraordinary: the Gospel.

~110~

Some months ago, a cousin of my wife Vida asked me:

"How can I know what God wants from me?" At some point in our lives, we all ask ourselves the same question. At 48 years old, I discovered that God does not ask us for anything extraordinary, nor does He impose burdens beyond our capacity.

Do you think God imposes too many burdens on you? "If you knew the gift of God." (John 4:10) He does everything for our good. All that's left is for you to let Him act in your life. He is a close God. "For in Him we live and move and have our being." (Acts 17:28)

Our intelligence is limited, and we will never fully understand the supernatural, the works, and the motives of God. But we can be sure, at all times, that God loves us immensely, and that we are special to Him.

~111~

I've been reflecting for days on what God wants from each of us, and it's not easy to find answers. Some are very clear and evident. Others are engraved in the human heart. God speaks to us. Do you want to listen?

From the beginning, He spoke to humanity and made His precepts known. Just open the Bible to find them.

'Listen to my voice, and I will be your God, and you shall be my people. Walk in the way that I command you, so that it may go well with you.' (Jeremiah 7:23)

What does God ask of us?

That we love Him.

The passage of God leaves your soul with a sweet hope. It ignites your heart. It fills you with tenderness and peace. You regain joy. You understand in that moment why so many men and women have decided and continue to decide for God. They spent and spent their lives for something great and extraordinary.

I always remember that good priest who doubted. He thought about leaving the priesthood and went on retreat to reflect and reconsider. One afternoon, under the shade of a tree, he cried out: 'What do you want from me, Lord? Who am I to you?' Then, a gentle breeze enveloped him, and he heard with the clarity of the wind a kind voice saying to him: 'You are mine.' He then understood the wonder of his calling, his belonging to God, and decided to continue.

I also remember that man who was diagnosed with terminal cancer. He was young and had a family. The day he was notified, he took his car and drove until dawn. In the car, he cried out: 'Why me? Why me?' Suddenly, a great peace flooded his soul, and he felt a gentle voice whispering from the back seat: 'Do not fear, I am with you.' I thought of these verses from Psalm 27: 'Wait for the Lord; be strong and take heart and wait for the Lord.'"

~113~

"As God knows our hearts, He left us His commandments. He knows we need them to be happy.

The 10 Commandments:

1. You shall love God above all things.
2. You shall not take the name of God in vain.
3. Remember to keep holy the Lord's Day.
4. Honor your father and mother.
5. You shall not kill.
6. You shall not commit adultery.
7. You shall not steal.
8. You shall not bear false witness against your neighbor.
9. You shall not covet your neighbor's wife.
10. You shall not covet your neighbor's goods.

A good priest once said:

"Imagine living in a community where the commandments are respected and followed. At night, when it's time to go to sleep, you wouldn't have to close the doors or windows of your homes because there is a commandment that says, 'You shall not steal.' You could also go out at any time you like to go anywhere, because there is a commandment that says, 'You shall not kill.'"

These commandments are a blessing. Jesus brought them to their fullness:

"I give you a new commandment: love one another. As I have loved you, so you also should love one another." (John 13:34-35)

There is a special promise with this commandment: "If you keep my commandments, you will remain in my love, just as I have kept my Father's commandments and remain in his love." (John 15:9)

This call from Jesus is so complete and wonderful that St. Augustine said:

"Love and do what you will."

~114~

Besides making known His Will to us, God reveals to each of us a personal, very intimate mission. It's like an inner voice that tells you what to do with your life, what God expects from you. Have you ever felt it? Have you asked Him: "Lord, what do you want from me?"

It's the vocation. A calling that God makes to you from Eternity. The path you must follow to give meaning and fulfillment to your life.

There are so many paths in the world: Which one will I follow?

I know they all have a common way, a single destination: "love."

~115~

When I have any concerns, I cross the street and talk with my neighbor, Father Francisco. Last night, after leaving work, I stopped by to see him and asked him this question:

"How do you choose a safe path? How do you know what God wants from each person?"

He listened attentively to my concerns and replied, "In the Sacred Scriptures, we find a universal call to life. A call from God for us to be holy. This is fundamental: to save ourselves. To reach a glorious eternity."

Because "God desires all men to be saved and to come to the knowledge of the truth" (1 Timothy 2:4).

Then he gave me a recipe for becoming holy. It's quite simple: "Fulfill your little duty of each moment. Do what you must. It's in what you do." Then he continued, "Naturally propose concrete things, offering them out of love for Jesus. You can write them down in your agenda or on a piece of paper and stick them where you can see and remember them. Here are some examples: I will finish the work I started. I will use my time wisely. I will get up at the exact time my alarm goes off. I will show charity to everyone."

~116~

I remember reading about this man who was an engineer. Every morning he attended Mass, received the sacraments, and was honest in his work. He was a simple man, invisible to the world. Upon his death, the Pope beatified him. His housekeeper, upon hearing this, complained, "Why? All he did was fulfill his daily duties."

That's precisely why he was a saint. By fulfilling his daily obligations, he stamped them with a characteristic seal: "The Love of Christ."

Holiness resides in the simple, the everyday. There's no need to seek difficult or unattainable formulas. Just infuse our small daily works with love. We'll never know how much we can impact others' lives this way. Doing our little deeds, pleasing to God. Believe me, it's worth it!

A priest said in his sermon, "If we knew the celebration God has prepared for us in Heaven, we would all be saints of altars."

~117~

Do you not feel worthy of God's love? Is there anyone who is? Saint Josemaria Escriva has a wonderful phrase on this: "You feel unworthy? Well then... strive to become worthy. And that's it." See, it's that simple.

There's no need to be perfect either. The great saints had many flaws that they overcame as they drew closer to God and lived in His loving presence. God rewards the effort, the desire to become holy, the struggle to live your faith. You don't have to be worthy to follow God's call. He didn't choose us because we are worthy, but because He sees something special in us, perhaps He looks at us with the eyes of Love.

Yes, we are special to God.

As my friend Father Marco Antonio used to say, "A saint is not someone who never falls, but one who always gets up."

It's true, we must fight. To rise again and again. If they could do it, we can too. We have advantages in this battle because we are not alone. We have on our side God the Father, Holy Mary, all the saints in Heaven, our Guardian Angel, our Mother the Church, and Jesus in the Eucharist. And to strengthen us? Prayer and the sacraments.

~118~

Open your heart to divine inspirations. Learn to recognize God's Will in your life.

Chiara Lubich used to say, "Learn to listen to the voice of God deep within your soul, the voice of conscience; it will tell you what God wants from you in each moment."

Remember: "God expects more from you."

~119~

I think I've already told you. My best friend is named Jesus. I love visiting Him at noon, after lunch, in a chapel near my workplace. I find Him in the Tabernacle like a prisoner of love. He is there for us. The chapel is so quiet and welcoming. It invites prayer and contemplation. There, Jesus in the Blessed Sacrament always awaits me. We talk. We accompany each other for a while. He listens to me, and I listen to Him in the silence.

Sometimes I find myself complaining about things that happen to me. Today, I must confess, I went to complain again. When I knelt down, my cellphone rang. I left the chapel to answer it. It was a friend who hosts a radio program on a Catholic station. They wanted to interview me and broadcast it live.

"Well, aren't you amazing," I said to Jesus, smiling at His timing.

It's as if He said affectionately: "Alright, alright... stop complaining and get to work."

And that's what I did. I seized the opportunity and talked about Him and His Mercy, and how good He is to us. I never cease to be amazed by the things of Jesus.

~120~

Sometimes a reader of one of my books writes to me, asking: "If God is so good, why does He allow this catastrophe? If God is so good, why does this illness exist?" I have been tempted to reply: "Seek Him and you will understand. Because those who seek God, find Him. He meets us before we even begin to walk. The truth is, there are many things I do not understand and perhaps never will."

Over the years, I have stopped questioning. I have learned to recognize the paternal presence of God in my life. This is enough for me. I need nothing more. To trust even when things don't seem to make sense. To trust despite everything. To trust in my Heavenly Father.

There is a psalm that I love. I find comfort and hope in it: "When anxiety was great within me, your consolation brought me joy."

~121~

Sometimes, when I feel like I can't go on, I simply leave things in God's hands. He always knows what to do. At that moment, an inner strength arises within me, a tender and pure love, that drives me forward, that keeps me from faltering. And I start again, with the joy of knowing I am loved, that I am special to God.

~122~

"Go into all the world and proclaim the Good News to every creature."
Mark 16:15

A few days ago, I asked a catechist: "What does God want from us?" "He wants us to do His holy will," he replied. "And what is His will?" "That we live the Gospel and proclaim it." "That's true," I thought. "Our world is tired of so many words. We need people who dare to live the Gospel. Modern saints: executives, traders, workers, secretaries, doctors... They should show us it's possible, like St. Francis of Assisi did in his time and Mother Teresa of Calcutta in ours.

~123~

Saint Josemaria Escriva used to say: "World crises are crises of holiness." And I wondered: "What would our world be like if Christians lived the Gospel? Surely, we would have a piece of heaven here on earth. A spiritual oasis. A refuge for humanity."

~124~

A friend has left everything behind to live her ideal within a movement of the Catholic Church. She left her job, comforts, family, and moved to another country. Yesterday we had a chance to talk, and I took the opportunity to ask her:

"How did you know what God was asking of you?" "There are many signs, but above all, there is a certainty in the heart that one wants to spend life for something great."

"How do you know how to interpret them?" "Through prayer. Prayer is more than just praying. It's a relationship with someone you love. That's why it involves our entire life. In other words, if you love someone, you do many things for that person. It's the same with God, and the more love moves me, the deeper that relationship becomes. Then, that voice that once called us will become clear and strong. Only by loving can one understand God's call."

She reminded me of the words of Blessed Charles de Foucauld: "At the same moment that I believed that God existed, I understood that I could not do anything else but live for Him.

~125~

Words of Jesus for you:

"Have you realized?
You are special to me."

~126~

"Everything he does is timely; yet he has placed eternity in their hearts, without men grasping the whole scope of what God is doing from beginning to end."

Ecclesiastes 3:11

The priest said in his homily today:
"Let us bear fruits of eternity,
because we are called to eternity."

~127~

Today everything speaks to us about God. Cheer up! You're going to do great. You're going to have a wonderful day. The best day of your life.

~128~

Do you want answers?

Start loving, and God will respond to you.

~129~

THOUGHTS

- When you live in the world, things get complicated. That's when God's "grace" intervenes. And what seemed impossible becomes possible.
- There are many steps to reach heaven. One, obedience; another, purity; another, humility; and a very important one: pain, suffering, so difficult to climb. But the most beautiful one is Love.
- Do you have a crucifix? Embrace it! Embrace it tightly and comfort our Lord.
- Have you spent a night in prayer? The soul unites with God and there is such a strong, sweet feeling...
- Grace is not always with you. Sometimes it withdraws, testing your faith. You no longer feel that peace, that joy. You feel abandoned in the middle of the desert. And now it all depends on you. Jesus, by your side, watches over you like a mother and father, ready to give you a hand. The mother must let go of the child so that they learn to walk. Jesus does the same with us.
- Our problems are nothing compared to the immensity and mercy of God.

~130~

Jesus, comfort of souls,
comfort me.

I suffer and I need you.

Stay with me.
Do not abandon me.

Give me your grace,
your love, and strength.

You can't imagine how much God favors us. Even in the smallest, everyday things. Everything is important to Him.

~131~

Have you seen those movies with great battles where a soldier is wounded and lies helpless in the midst of the battlefield? Bullets whistle around him. Mortars explode. And he cannot move.

Suddenly, a heroic soldier runs to his rescue. He risks everything and reaches his side. He picks him up and runs back to safety. That's how we should be, heroes of God. Risking everything for souls in danger, those wounded by sin. Praying for them, asking God for the grace of their conversion, that they may be saved.

How serious is our sin of omission when we abandon them to their fate.

~132~

Around our world, millions of people have chosen love and strive to live the Gospel. They have hope for a better life. They confront themselves, fighting a battle that fills them with courage and faith.

Others see them without understanding. To them, it's inexplicable. "And these people? Why are they so happy?" they anxiously question. They are the ones who think there is no Heaven, no Purgatory, no Hell. They mock the Sacraments, the Holy Mass, holy water, Marian devotions. They seem like fearful children who have lost the path to salvation. They do not realize the enormous danger they have exposed themselves to. Others simply have no interest in these matters. "Someday I'll go to Confession," they say, thinking that moment will come. They are naive. I know of many who did not have this opportunity. They died in mortal sin, suddenly.

Jesus looks upon us with compassion and smiles kindly. He knows there is no reason to fear. If souls knew Him, they would not hesitate to surrender to His Mercy. They would run to seek the Father, knowing themselves citizens of heaven, children of a great King.

~133~

How to respond to a God who loves us so much?

The answer is known to you: by loving Him above all else — loving Him amidst adversity, amidst misunderstandings ... Always loving one another and loving God above all things.

~134~

Our life with God is based on trust. God delights in your trust in Him.

At my age, I have learned something fundamental:

- If you trust greatly, you receive greatly.
- If you trust little, you receive little.

God gives to you according to your trust. And to teach you to trust, He takes you like a father with a young child learning to walk. He holds your hand, filling you with abundant graces. Suddenly, unexpectedly, you feel filled with God, with immense happiness that overflows. And you long to share it with others.

You begin to see the miracles that you didn't notice before. A sunrise, the rain, a child's gaze, a stone.

You live on grace to then live on faith.

~135~

What prevents God from dwelling within you?

- Fear.
- Distrust.
- Greed.
- Attachment to material things.
- Greed.
- Envy.
- Laziness.
- Lust.
- Pride.
- Arrogance.
- Hatreds.
- Mortal sins.

Do you see yourself reflected in any of these sins? I do, often. That's why it's beneficial to visit the confessional regularly. Cleanse your soul and make room for God.

Your soul is too precious to lose.

~136~

The other day I was thinking: "How does God feel dwelling within me?" Truthfully, I saw Him traveling on a fifth-class bus. Without comforts. That day, I went to confession. I left feeling happy, knowing it was a new opportunity God was giving me. Happy because I longed to provide God with a decent place to dwell. As Saint Paul said: "Do you not know that you are a temple of God and that the Spirit of God dwells in you?" (1 Corinthians 3:16)

I imagined Jesus with a broom sweeping every corner of my soul. With His broom, He swept out all sorts of dead vermin. He looked at me again with a gesture of admonishment yet deep love, and said to me, "Do you see what I do for you?"

~137~

Today we will do something different. Do you have a Bible at home? Look for it, you will need it. What I am about to tell you will mark a before and after in your life. Did you know that the sin by which most souls are lost and go to hell is the sin of the flesh? Adultery seems to be something common. "What do you advise us, Claudio?" Read 1 Corinthians 6:18-20. It explains it clearly: "Flee from sexual immorality. All other sins a person commits are outside the body, but whoever sins sexually, sins against their own body. Do you not know that your bodies are temples of the Holy Spirit, who is in you, whom you have received from God? You are not your own; you were bought at a price. Therefore honor God with your bodies." 1 Corinthians 6:18-20

Now, what are these sins of the flesh so terrifying that they can condemn us for eternity? Open your Bible to Galatians 5 and read verses 19-21, so that there are no doubts, and you can say, "I did not know." "It is easy to recognize what comes from the flesh: sexual immorality, impurity, and debauchery; idolatry and witchcraft; hatred, discord, jealousy, fits of rage, selfish ambition, dissensions, factions and envy; drunkenness, orgies, and the like. I warn you, as I did before, that those who live like this will not inherit the kingdom of God." We are warned. No one will be able to say they did not know.

~138~

Everything is based on trust. And God will always give you reasons to do so.

~139~

What should you do to move forward and find personal peace? It's time to pray, be silent, listen to Jesus, and trust. Above all, lead a life of prayer.

I've realized how important prayer is, praying before the Blessed Sacrament, praying alongside Jesus in the Tabernacle, praying with Jesus.

It excites Him when you accompany Him. He loves it when you visit. He becomes happy just to see you arrive.

Prayer strengthens you, allows you to be in God's loving presence, and is the remedy for many of our concerns. When I feel worried or uneasy, I pray. And as the minutes pass, I regain inner peace, the joy of knowing I am a beloved child of God.

~140~

I know I'm a bit naive and perhaps that's why I'm not the best person to give advice. I'm clear about that. In my books, you'll find personal experiences, testimonies of faith, miracles I've witnessed. With that information, you decide what you'll do with your life. No one can live for you. The truth is that life is wonderful, a precious gift given to us to cherish.

What goals are meaningful to you? What would you like to do with your life? What would move you to give your best effort? Write down 3 important dreams to conquer, goals, aspirations, hopes that you are willing to fight for, strive for, persevere in, and change your life for.

1.

2.

3.

Now go and make them a reality.

~141~

Every time someone asks me about the effectiveness of prayer, I remember the story of Harry, a taxi driver I met on a rainy July morning at a workshop. He was a short, sturdy man who somehow exuded a lot of peace. I was the manager of the place, and he approached me to ask about some tools for his car. We ended up chatting. He told me about the nightmare and miracle he had just experienced three nights earlier while working in his taxi.

"I picked up a young couple in love outside a movie theater. They put a gun to my head and threatened to shoot if I didn't give them money and take them to an address. As I became nervous, the girl, more aggressive, shouted uncontrollably, 'He saw our faces. Kill him, Rubén! What are you waiting for?' I felt scared. I thought I was going to die that night. I am a religious man and decided to surrender myself into God's hands and face my executioner calmly in prayer. I began to pray aloud: 'Lord, do not hold this sin against them, honor your servant, protect me as I take refuge in you.'

The young man shouted to his friend, 'Don't you see? He is a servant of God. We can't touch him.' He looked at me fearfully and ordered, 'Stop the car here.' I did as he asked, and they both got out of the taxi without harming me or taking my money.

~142~

Do you know the psalms? There are 150 in total. It's soul-stirring to know that Jesus also prayed with the psalms. In fact, on the cross, these words come from Psalm 22: 'My God, my God, why have you forsaken me?' I like to pray with them. There's one in particular expressing trust in God's protection and care (Psalm 121) that has always moved and strengthened me when I go through great difficulty.

My eyes are lifted up to the hills:
O where will my help come from?
Your help comes from the Lord,
who made heaven and earth.
May he not let your foot be moved:
no need of sleep has he who keeps you.
See, the eyes of Israel's keeper will not be shut in sleep.
The Lord is your keeper; t
he Lord is your shade on your right hand.
You will not be touched by the sun in the day,
or by the moon at night.
The Lord will keep you safe from all evil;
he will take care of your soul.
The Lord will keep watch
over your going out and your coming in,
from this time and forever.

~143~

What have I learned from prayer? I know that without it we are lost, we weaken, and easily succumb to temptations. Jesus taught us what is important in prayer. You can read it in Matthew 21, 22: 'And whatever you ask in prayer, you will receive, if you have faith.' Therefore, for prayer to be effective, it must be accompanied by:

1. Faith.
2. Perseverance.
3. Love.
4. Trust.
5. Humility.

~144~

With age and life experiences, you understand that everything boils down to something so simple, so straightforward that it seems unbelievable:

'God loves us.'

That's it. There's no need to search for anything more. God loves us. With a love so great, undeserved, immense, and infinite that we cannot measure it or fully comprehend it.

I have seen His wonders in everyday life. Every day. Every morning. That's why, gladly, I would shout like the psalmist, so that everyone could hear me:

'The Lord has been great to us.'

~145~

Today I have lived immersed in the waters of God. Enamored with His Love. I nourish myself with His Love. And I am deeply moved beyond words. Those who see me from the outside wouldn't know what's happening, because it's something so intimate and internal. I stay in a corner enjoying these moments. Without moving, without speaking. Just experiencing His loving presence.

I still don't know how to describe this experience; I often say it happens when God passes by. And everything is transformed.

~146~

When things aren't going well, I tell myself:

'It's true, only God is enough. Trust, Claudio. You must trust.'

And suddenly, unexpectedly, everything gets resolved. The value of trust is immense in the eyes of God. I've realized that if we trust deeply, we receive much. If we trust little, we receive little. We must trust, no matter how dark the situation may seem.

'Lord, teach me to trust.'

~147~

I received a letter from a young woman in which she said, 'They mock me because I go to Mass. It seems like the young people in my neighborhood no longer believe in God.'

I don't know why, but I felt compelled to respond from the heart: 'Well, you already have a ministry. And a wonderful one at that. Be a light in your neighborhood. Illuminate the paths to God with the example of your life.'

'But what should I do?' she asked anxiously.

'Nothing,' I replied. 'God will do everything. Just live the Gospel. Be holy. Your example in everyday life will be enough to touch their lives and illuminate them. Ask the Good Lord to make you His instrument, and He will. God is good.

~148~

I know. I might seem foolish, naive, but I lost my fear of what others might say a long time ago. It's not that I don't care, but there's something greater that drives me to live this way; to write and speak about God. Long ago, I understood that even if I wanted to stay silent, I couldn't. God has impacted my life. Over the years, I've come to recognize His loving presence.

I love reading biographies of those who have had crucial moments in their lives. It's incredible how God shows up. Where there were doubts, faith remains. Where there was anguish, peace remains.

From now on, be very careful not to offend a God who is our Father in heaven, so good and tender. These words spring from my soul, as a plea of love.

'May the words of my mouth and the thoughts and desires of my heart be pleasing to you, Lord.'

~149~

I experience the same as you. It's natural, we're people with feelings. Sometimes I get discouraged and say to myself, 'No more.' But I keep going, driven by a force that isn't mine. And in the end, I recognize that this effort, my desire for holiness, is worthwhile. God is always worthwhile.

I went through what Jeremiah did, who at one point in his life wanted to give it all up. But God ignited his heart and soul; He didn't abandon him. He accompanied him and protected him.

'Therefore, I said, "I will not mention his word, nor speak any more in his name," but his word was in my heart like a burning fire shut up in my bones; I was weary with forbearing, and I could not endure it.' (Jeremiah 20:9)

Believe me, it's wonderful to return to God's paths. To live in His loving presence.

It's always worthwhile to follow God.

~150~

God spoils His children, and sometimes we don't even have to ask. He knows in advance what we need.

I always remember with emotion the time I left work and found that students had closed the streets, protesting the high cost of living. I couldn't get home for lunch. 'How much I would like a homemade meal,' I thought. So, I drove to a place where they sell sandwiches. On the way, I saw a Franciscan nun waiting for a taxi. Since her convent was behind the place where I worked, I offered to give her a ride, and she gladly accepted. She asked me how things were going, and I told her about the adventures of that midday.

'Why don't you come to the convent and have lunch with us?' she kindly suggested.

'Really?' I asked, surprised.

'Of course!' she exclaimed, smiling.

And there I was, enjoying a delicious homemade meal, surrounded by those sweet nuns. Just what I had wished for.

~151~

This morning I went to visit Jesus in the Blessed Sacrament. I try to go often. I love being with Him. I entered this small chapel, which feels like a foretaste of heaven. You see Him and He looks at you. Gratefully, I thought about my family, my children, and the gift of life. Suddenly, I felt as if Jesus was asking me: 'Tell them that I love them.' I know He loves you and loves us. I see it every day. I live it every day. That's why I know.

'Jesus loves you.'

~152~

In the world, there are many paths of perdition that lead you away from God, suffocate you, and tie you to a world that is fleeting, temporary. That's why you lose the strength of faith, hope, and don't know what to do with your life. The pleasure of some sins lasts very briefly, and you could lose your soul for all eternity. On October 13, 1917, the Virgin Mary at Fatima warned us about our behavior: 'Do not offend Our Lord God anymore, for He is already very offended.' I often recommend to people who feel the need to draw closer to God and change their lives some very simple actions within their reach: Make a good sacramental confession to reconcile yourself with God. Seek advice from a priest experienced in spiritual life. You need a spiritual director to guide you and help you progress in your inner life, in that closeness to God which we all need to be happy. Visit Jesus in the tabernacle frequently. Stay in adoration. Ask Him for the graces you need to strengthen your soul. He often has all the answers you are seeking. Read books on spirituality. You need to know the doctrine and see the example left by the saints of our Church. There's a book I often recommend titled 'The Story of a Soul.' It was written by Saint Thérèse of Lisieux. *"It is a spiritual classic and is one of the most beautiful autobiographies ever written"*. You can find it at any Catholic bookstore near your home. But remember always, the most important book is the Holy Bible.

~153~

Which path to take? The answer is in the Holy Bible. And it's very simple. You can find it in John 14:6: 'I am the way, the truth, and the life.' The secure path is Jesus. Follow His footsteps through an evangelical life. In other words, strive to live the Gospel.

God's love for humanity is so great that He not only places an Angel to guard us throughout life's journey but also sends His Son, and as if that weren't enough, leaves us with hundreds of promises.

I've read that there are over 3,000 promises of God in the Bible. And each and every one of them is fulfilled.

'Blessed rather are those who hear the Word of God and obey it.' (Luke 11:28)

Of all His promises, this is one of the most impressive to me:

'Ask and it will be given to you; seek and you will find; knock and the door will be opened to you. For everyone who asks receives; the one who seeks finds; and to the one who knocks, the door will be opened.' (Matthew 7:7-8)

How good you are, Lord, our God and Father, who loves us infinitely, despite what we do and who we are.

~154~

When I was young, I read a book that impressed me deeply. It was titled 'Seeking God' by Guy de Laurigaudie. Years have passed, and even today I remember some of its passages and reflections. They have helped me to draw closer to God.

'Many live almost without sin. Their lives unfold smoothly within the ordinary framework of their work, their family. They fulfill God's will through the main obligations of their daily lives. But their existence seems ordinary, cold, without light; they lack the love of God. They are like well-built houses, but without fire. They are good, but not holy. One must have the heart completely filled with God, as a lover's heart is filled with the woman he loves.' Today, while driving the car, I was thinking about this. It took many years to fully understand that reflection. I would have liked to be holy, to please God, to live immersed in His love. As a child, my greatest aspiration was to have a pure heart, to be holy to please God. I am one who has lived seeking God, but without going further, without taking that step that brings us closer to His love, without full trust, without abandonment. I understood what I lack: 'Having the heart completely filled with God.' That has been the difference between someone good and a saint... A little more love, just a bit more. It's like a boundary we dare not cross due to comfort and fear, uncertainty, distrust. I would like to take that step, to go further, to trust completely, to live in God's hands. Everything would be different for me.

~155~

I have seen some people who have dared to change their lives for love of God. In their eyes shines excitement; they spread peace, hope, happiness everywhere they go. They are always joyful, and in their presence, you experience the presence of God. You know that God is within them.

I hope you also dare to cross this border and choose God. Let's do it together. Let's cross as a group, let's live for God, in His love. Imagine the face of God when a multitude decides to live in holiness, and together we reach the promised Paradise.

Often, I meet people who ask me if God loves them, if we are special to Him. They go through so many difficulties that it's hard for them to believe there is a God who is Father and who lovingly watches over us and loves us from eternity. In two days, I will turn 67 years old. Life hasn't been easy for me. Writing these books hasn't exempted me from suffering and going through life's turbulence. I have had to strive hard to support my family, and I have always had the support of my wife Vida. Together, we have lived great adventures with God. Difficulties and adversity have not been lacking. Every time I found myself at one of these crossroads where I didn't know which way to turn, I would retreat to reflect and pray. I would think:

'If I keep my state of grace, God will dwell in me, as we are temples of the Holy Spirit. This way, I can make the right decisions.'

Somewhere I read: 'God and I, we are a majority.' And it has its reasons because God is Almighty. In the end, I always chose the right path, the one that would lead me to conquer my goals. I realized that we have many paths before us, and almost daily we must choose. I choose God and His infinite love; I choose hope, joy, faith, family life, love, and forgiveness. And you?

~157~

Sometimes Jesus touches our hearts. It's very warm and tender. I know Him well, and I know when it's Him. You don't fully understand in the moment what is happening. It's an unheard-of happiness, like a longing you've fulfilled. I know Jesus has also touched your soul at some point. Pay attention to Him. Listen to Him.

Many years ago, I heard that life is like traveling on a tram. You're headed towards a destination, and along the way, the tram stops at different stations. Some people get on, others get off. Many who board become part of your life, then they disembark, never to be seen again. Some ride quietly, and you don't realize they traveled with you. Others, over the years, reappear and you reconnect with them. When I first boarded a tram, I couldn't imagine the adventures I would have, the beautiful landscapes passing before me, the endless search I would begin. I was a child and only lived in the present. The world was incomprehensible to me, like a blank canvas.

Life is a great adventure and it's meant to be lived. Life is also short. I have strived to live it with my family, doing what I am passionate about: writing.

I often wonder if it was worth it. Interestingly, every time I have concerns and ask myself that question, the answer isn't far off. It's just around the corner. It happened to me a few days ago. I was at Mass, setting up a table outside with my books. I felt tired and wondered if it was worth it. At that moment, a lady who came out of the chapel of the Blessed Sacrament approached me, bought one of my books, and said, 'It's worth it, keep doing it.'

~158~

God is the best passenger I've had on the tram of my life, the most remarkable and also the quietest. He travels silently, almost unnoticed, attentive to everything. I am certain that He has been present in every moment of my life, accompanying me, watching over us, guiding us like a child, showing us the scenery through the window. There are extraordinary moments when you look at the sky and say, 'Thank you. I know it was you.'

The truth is that God never abandons you.

I heard about a young mountaineer who slipped and hung for hours on the edge of a cliff. He pleaded with God for another chance. 'Help me, Lord,' he implored. When he was rescued, the first thing he said was, 'God exists.' The rescuer, deeply impressed, replied, 'Yes, God exists.'

I didn't know how to begin. This book is very special to me. Suddenly, I thought of God and His infinite love, and I knew that my first word would be His holy and magnificent name: 'God.'

Don't you find His Name beautiful?

It is He who tells you, 'You are special to Me.'

~159~

Today I went out early for a walk. With every step, I thought, 'Sometimes we walk on the edge of the precipice for You, Lord, and often we don't know what to do. We just keep walking, thinking of Your Love, Your presence. What do You want from us? Suddenly You immerse us in a world where we don't wish to be. It's a dark place, full of difficulties. It seems there's no love or hope around us. These are situations where we find no way out. Every time I tell You this, I feel You respond: "Keep walking."

You can't imagine the number of people who tell me their problems. They come to me maybe because they've read one of my books. They live surrounded by darkness. It usually impresses me. And I ask, 'Why do You allow it? Why this suffering?' Many years ago, I decided to stop questioning and to trust instead. How could we understand You, we who are mere mortals? But the truth is, I haven't always been able to stay calm and trust.

Today is one of those days when I am filled with concerns. Curiously, while I walked, I seemed to find the answers. All these people, because they are immersed in their problems, forgot something fundamental: what they really are—Your children. Bearers of Your Love. Messengers of Hope. It's a seal we will never lose. We are little lights You place in these terrible places to illuminate them. We don't realize it, burdened by difficulties. You want us to carry You to others, to be Your arms, Your feet, Your voice.

If we were aware of what You expect from us, everything would be simpler. We could forgive and love. Embrace the needy. Perhaps we need the certainty of a purpose to embrace hope and spread it throughout the world.

I don't know why I'm telling You these things. Suddenly I found the answer in my Bible, and I understood completely: 'You are the light of the world. A city set on a hill cannot be hidden; nor does anyone light a lamp and put it under a basket, but on the lampstand, and it gives light to all who are in the house. Let your light shine before men in such a way that they may see your good works and glorify your Father who is in heaven.' (Matthew 5:13-16).

I always remember that young woman who one morning came to my office to submit her resignation. 'Has someone treated you badly?' I asked, surprised. 'On the contrary,' she replied, 'everyone has been very kind to me.' 'Then why are you leaving?' I asked, puzzled. She smiled enthusiastically and said, 'It's because I am pursuing an ideal. I want to spend my life on something great, something that truly matters.'

Years later, I met her outside Mass and asked, 'Was it worth it?' She was radiant and replied excitedly, 'I would do it a thousand times over if I could be born again. It is always worth living for God.'

The answer is clear now. We must be the light that illuminates others. Show them the way to lead them to You. But we are a weak, faint candle. How can we make it shine again? It's very easy. Jesus tells you:

'Reclaim grace. Have a life of prayer. Do good deeds. Live in Me... and I will be your light.'

~161~

This morning something curious happened to me. On my way to work, I was thinking with regret about what I could have been but wasn't. 'If only I had become a doctor,' I reproached myself, 'I could have saved many lives,' and I continued with these thoughts for a while. I passed by the church around the corner from my workplace, as I do every morning, stopped for a few seconds, greeted Jesus, and continued on my way. Then, everything became so clear and evident. I seemed to understand God's will and began to reflect. What does God want from us? Does He want us to give lectures? Does He want us to do many things in His name? He seeks something so simple, yet surprising. God desires our love. This is enough for Him. He asks for nothing more. Our poor love as imperfect humans. That's why He gave us this commandment: 'You shall love the Lord your God with all your heart, with all your soul, and with all your strength.' Our most important task is love. If you love, you will discover God in your brothers and sisters, in the poor, the rich, the suffering, the elderly, the children... and you will live in His loving and holy presence. The one who loves has conquered the best part, because God is love. Can you love God with all your heart? This is an amazing grace that I have always admired in the saints and that I frequently pray for. For me, it is a bit challenging to love without measure, to love as God asks.

~162~

Dear God,

Recently, I was praying with that beautiful prayer of St. Francis: "Lord, make me an instrument of your peace." I felt transported to paradise, filled with inner joy. I wanted to go through the world being an instrument of peace. Later, a car cut me off at a corner, and without thinking, I uttered unspeakable words at the driver. Immediately, I remembered Francis' prayer and felt ashamed, thinking to myself, "what an instrument of peace I am."

I recognized that we are made of clay, and it came from my soul to say, "Lord, make us truly instruments of your peace.

~163~~

Often I wonder about the meaning of life. "Why are we here?" "What does God want from us?" Has it ever happened to you? It happens to me frequently. I try to understand the whys of life. On days like these when I pause and reflect, I like to remember this thought from St. Alberto Hurtado that helps me understand: "Why are we in the world? We are in the world because someone loved us: God. We are in the world to love and to be loved."

There are some important things you should know. Even in the midst of affliction, He is with you. His love for you is immense. You are not in the world by chance. God has a PLAN for you. He wants you to be happy. Do not be afraid. Surrender yourself to His Love. Trust in Him.

In His Love, He has left you many signs and visible signs hoping that you will discover the way that is Jesus. He knows that your life will be beneficial, you will achieve your dreams and goals. Some of these signals are in sight, right in front of you. And we often let them pass for fear of commitment. Cheer up! God expects more from you.

~164~

Do you want to change your life? You already know the Way. It's right there in front of you. "Here I am," Jesus says to you, "I AM THE WAY. Do not be afraid." You are filled with an inexplicable joy, a peace that is not of this world, a serenity that helps you face your problems and emerge victorious. Live in grace. Live in His Presence. And the world will change for you. Everything will be different. In those moments, a gesture of tenderness will come from your soul, and you will say:

"I love you Jesus. I love you. And I will always love you."

~165~

During my childhood in the city of Colon, I studied at a small, welcoming Franciscan school. Sweet nuns taught us our classes. I remember being quite distracted, but I lived with excitement the stories and lives of saints they told us, as if walking alongside the characters.

There was a song that I loved, and I've just heard it again today. You probably know it. It began like this:

"Oh Mary, my Mother, oh comfort of mortals, protect me and guide me to the celestial Homeland."

There's also a consecration that I still make today, imploring her protection.

Oh my Lady! Oh my Mother! I offer myself entirely to you and as a token of my filial affection, I consecrate to you on this day, my eyes, my ears, my tongue, my heart; in a word, my whole being.

Since I am all yours, oh Mother of goodness, keep me and defend me as your possession and property.

Amen.

~166~

Life is often difficult for everyone. Things don't always turn out as we expect, and we often fall and struggle to get back up. It happens to me frequently. It's natural; we are mere humans. We are in need of His Mercy and His Love. Have you lost your way? Then take courage and reclaim it. These are the moments when you must pray and implore with fervor for mercy and forgiveness. There's a particular prayer that is very effective for these cases. It's "the prayer of Jesus." It's like a short, wonderful ejaculation, and I love to repeat it: "Jesus, Son of God, have mercy on me, a sinner." Pray with confidence. Be assured that He will always listen to you. Don't be anxious. Know Jesus. Live for Jesus. I love knowing that Jesus is my friend. You can't imagine how thrilled I am that He is my best friend, my GREAT friend. I don't want to offend Him. That's why when I fall, I usually confess as soon as possible. I listen attentively to the advice of the good priest. In the confessional, I tell myself: "Listen, Jesus is going to speak to you through him." I have received the best advice from them. I often say to them: "Thank you for being a priest." I also have my Bible close by. Do you have one near you? Open it and read the Beatitudes carefully. There's one that has impressed me greatly. It's beautiful. "Blessed are the pure in heart, for they shall see God." Can you believe it? To be able to see God. Finally getting to know Him, being in His Presence.

Saying to Him, "Father," and hearing Him respond tenderly, "My child, you have finally come home."

~167~

In life, we walk through a terrain filled with strong temptations. Jesus knew this and told us HOW TO TRIUMPH:

"*Watch and pray so that you will not fall into temptation. The spirit is willing, but the flesh is weak*" (Mt 26:41).

That's why Saint Felix advised: "Keep your eyes on the ground, your heart in heaven, and in your hands, the holy Rosary."

~168~

Your children are going down the wrong path? Don't worry. Did you know that a mother's prayer is powerful? God always listens to it with pleasure. We have the example of an extraordinary woman, Monica of Hippo. Have you heard of her? She was admirable, a role model for every mother who prays for her children. We know that "she was born in present-day Algeria. She married at a young age to an older man named Patricius. They had three children. Her husband was a violent man with libertine habits. Monica's good actions and prayers unsettled Patricius, yet he treated her with respect. Monica went to church daily and patiently endured her husband's adultery and anger. Through praying for him and making sacrifices, she converted Patricius to Christianity and calmed his violence. One of her sons was known for his debauchery, leading a joyful and dissipated life, named Augustine. For over 15 years, she prayed for his conversion without ceasing. Her prayers bore fruit. Augustine converted and changed his life. In time, he became ordained as a priest, was appointed bishop, and became known as the great Saint Augustine. "He is praised as the greatest of the Church Fathers." And all this was thanks to the persistence, prayers, and sacrifices of Saint Monica. Trust and keep praying for your child, even if you don't see immediate results. Your timing is not God's timing. He will know when the right time is. Persevere in prayer.

~169~

Prayer has power, undoubtedly, it makes God listen to us and obtain from Him what we need. Jesus assured this, which is no small thing. He didn't say, perhaps, who knows, it's possible. He said clearly: "Truly I tell you." Open your Bible, the one you have stored at home or on a wooden lectern. Look up Matthew 21 and read verses 21 and 22. It's a truly extraordinary promise. "Jesus answered them, 'Truly I tell you, if you have faith and do not doubt, not only can you do what was done to the fig tree, but also you can say to this mountain, "Go, throw yourself into the sea," and it will be done. If you believe, you will receive whatever you ask for in prayer.'"

Ask with faith and expect the best. God always acts in your favor. To pray, you must be in God's loving presence, attentive to His spiritual inspirations, His Words... for this, it is beneficial to examine our inner selves, to ask ourselves a very simple question: "Is there room for God in my life?" I remember that occasion after Mass when the priest invited us to pray with a psalm. We started aloud, most of us in a rush to finish quickly. The good priest stopped us. "Praying is not reciting, it is talking to God," he said with emotion. "Let's pray without haste, knowing that God sees us and hears us." So we started again, this time slowly, with the certainty that God was with us, listening to us.

~170~

Most of us get distracted while praying. I always remember with special affection this priest who told us a story about prayer, and I love sharing it whenever I can.

Two men met and made a bet. "I bet you this horse," he said, pointing to a beautiful colt, "that you can't pray the Our Father without getting distracted."

His friend thought the idea was great, confident that he would win, and began: "Our Father who art in heaven, hallowed be..." Here he interrupted the prayer and asked, "But the horse, is it saddled or unsaddled?"

It seems to me that it was Saint Basil who advised: "How will you overcome distractions in prayer? By seriously thinking that God is watching you."

~171~

There are anecdotes about prayer that I enjoy sharing. I have a friend at EWTN, Mother Angelica's Catholic Television Channel. Her name is Cristina Ramis.

A few years ago, I wrote to her sharing my reflections and asking about her experience with prayer. In time, she emailed me back sharing these uplifting stories:

"We receive daily testimonies of the power of prayer. These come from viewers and listeners who ask us to pray for their intentions, and then write or call us to thank God for granting what they needed. One viewer sent us an email requesting prayer for his mother who had suffered a stroke and could no longer speak. She is very elderly, 91 years old. At that age, one tends to think, 'Well, she has lived her life and the Lord will soon take her home to enjoy Paradise.' But here we always take the prayer intention and place it at the foot of the altar for 30 days.

About a month later, her son writes to thank us. Suddenly, his mother not only started speaking again, but also sings when visited by family and friends. Everyone is amazed... at 91 years old.

One of my favorite testimonies is from a distressed mother who wrote asking for prayer so that her husband and son would reconcile, as they had not spoken for two years. Immediately, we placed this intention at the altar and prayed, both the friars and the channel staff.

The lady writes back shortly after: 'Today, when I went to pick up the mail from the mailbox, I found your letter saying that you are praying for the reconciliation of my son and husband. As I stand at the door holding the letter, my son arrives in his car to reconcile with his father!'

~172~

Praying for another is to take their place, their burdens, to carry them together. It's approaching God as siblings, showing our concern for others.

A friend who lives dedicated to God, performing Works of Mercy where she lives, wrote to me sharing her testimony:

"Dear Claudio: The experience I have with intercessory prayer is one of humility and self-forgetfulness. It practices mercy, for praying for others is one of the most pleasing Works of Mercy to God, and it exercises the soul in the virtue of perfect love. There are many examples of Jesus interceding in prayer for us, forgetting about His own feelings and knowing what would happen by accepting the will of His Father God.

In my particular case, practicing intercessory prayer is a path of abandonment and trust, because what I need to ask Jesus for, He already knows! In this way, I exercise trust and abandonment. I practice love by thinking about and interceding for my brother."

~173~

Surely you wonder whom you can pray for. The world has a great need for your prayer. The list is endless. If you knew all the good you do with your prayer for others, you would never stop. You can pray for:

*Your children.
*Your husband.
*Your parents.
*If you are religious, for your community.
*Those who hurt me.
*The souls of the departed.
*The dying.
*Those whom I have harmed.
*Children and families.
*Those suffering from violence.
*The blessed souls in Purgatory.
*The Pope, the Church, and priests.
*The sick.
*Students and their teachers.
*Prostitutes, drug addicts, and alcoholics.
*Those incarcerated in prison.
*The conversion of great sinners.

~174~

"Be steadfast in prayer; remain watchful in it with thanksgiving." (Colossians 4:2)

What does prayer mean to you? An anonymous author wrote:

"*Prayer is not about asking for things but understanding that you need nothing more than the presence of God and resting in that dwelling filled with His qualities*."

For me, this is prayer. To abide in the presence of God, immersed in Him. To let Him act in my life, to dwell within me. To feel His daily "presence." To experience His Love and His Peace.

In such a state, the soul never ceases to praise and thank God for so many blessings, so much Love, and so much Tenderness. It's like the prayer of offering. You offer your day to God at the beginning of the day, and even if you forget amidst it, He continues to look at you with anticipation, joyfully satisfied by that beautiful prayer.

When we pray for one another, God becomes present as a loving Father who embraces us, listens to us tenderly, and grants us what we deeply long for.

~175~

Talking to God, that is prayer. Dialoguing, asking, thanking, pleading, contemplating. It's also living in His loving presence. Experiencing His tenderness. Choosing Him. Being with Him, in Him. Allowing Him to dwell within us, as temples of the Holy Spirit. It's an uninterrupted dialogue between the Father and His Son. Between God and you.

I have known people who live their lives as if in deep prayer. They are humble, simple, happy.

Sometimes, I simply ponder on the wonders that God has done for us. From my soul springs forth a very simple prayer, a simple: "Thank you, Father." In some way, I feel that He is pleased. I think all of us who are fathers or mothers know how pleasant it is to have a grateful child approach us with a loving hug and say, "I love you, Dad" or "I love you, Mom."

Prayer is similar. We are in a dialogue with our Heavenly Father, asking, pleading, thanking, or simply being in His loving presence.

Prayer is so important in our lives that Pope Benedict XVI has also called it "the breath of the soul."

~176~

Mother Teresa's Favorite Prayer

Dear Jesus, help me to spread Your fragrance everywhere I go. Flood my soul with Your spirit and life.
Penetrate and possess my whole being so utterly,
that my life may only be a radiance of Yours.
Shine through me, and be so in me
that every soul I come in contact with
may feel Your presence in my soul.
Let them look up and see no longer me,
but only Jesus!
Stay with me and then I shall begin to shine as You shine, so to shine as to be a light to others.
The light, O Jesus will be all from You; none of it will be mine; it will be you, shining on others through me.
Let me thus praise You the way You love best, by shining on those around me. Let me preach You without preaching, not by words but by my example, by the catching force of the sympathetic influence of what I do, the evident fullness of the love my heart bears to You.

Amen.

John Henry Newman

~177~

St. Therese of Lisieux taught us how not to complicate prayer. She said, "For me, prayer is a surge of the heart; it is a simple look turned toward heaven, it is a cry of recognition and of love, embracing both trial and joy."

And St. Padre Pio of Pietrelcina shows us the key to encountering prayer. It is so simple that it surprises: Abandonment, trust, and humility.

"The gift of prayer is in the hands of the Savior. The more you empty yourself, that is, of self-love and all carnal attachment, entering into holy humility, the more God will communicate Himself to your heart."

Think about what distances you from God, what things prevent you from approaching Him. And set them aside. That useless pride. That difficulty in forgiving.

~178~

Have you ever experienced this? I've asked myself many times. What is the best prayer? I had read that prayer was like building a bridge to God. I imagined myself walking on that bridge that would lead me to God. And I understood that it all begins with a first step. The solution was to take one step at a time. First crawling, then walking, and finally running. Whenever I've faced difficulty, I've gone to see Jesus in the Tabernacle. Over the years, I've learned that He always has the answers. Occasionally, people come to me and share the difficulties they're going through. I usually take a piece of paper and write a spiritual prescription. I fold the paper and tell them, "This is your prescription." Almost all the notes say the same thing: "Visit Jesus in the Tabernacle. He eagerly awaits you." Days later, many would return telling me how a brief visit, where they sat in silence, just accompanying Him, was enough to change their lives. And it's because Jesus never sends anyone away without an answer, without the graces needed to restart the journey. I've seen it again and again. That's how Jesus is. He loves to be visited, and even more, He loves to shower us with spiritual gifts. Saint Josemaria Escriva gives us a very practical solution when we don't know what to say to Jesus, how to pray, what to do: "You don’t know what to say to the Lord in prayer. You can't remember anything, and yet you would like to discuss many things with Him. Look: during the day, take some notes on the things you want to consider in God's presence. And then go to pray with those notes."

~179~

I have pondered much on these words from the Gospel:

"In God we live, move, and exist."

If praying is talking to God, then it shouldn't be so difficult. It's not like writing a letter and sending it by mail, or sending an email, or looking for someone in another country.

We have God within us. We are temples of the Holy Spirit.

That's why praying is so simple. God always sees us and hears us, He is always with us. Whatever I say, He hears it; whatever gesture of love, He sees it.

It impresses me to know that God dwells within us, that we are temples of the Holy Spirit, and that in this life, despite being made of clay, we are sustained by prayer.

~180~

If we do not pray, our hearts grow cold, we lose hope, and our closeness with God diminishes. I have known people who have been examples their entire lives and suddenly, overwhelmed by daily problems, they abandon prayer and fall away. St. Alphonsus recounts the case of a very holy monk named Justin. He was pious and fervent. One day he was brought before the presence of the Supreme Pontiff, Pope Eugene IV, who, impressed by his virtues, embraced him and seated him beside him. Upon returning to the monastery, the monk began to feel that he was not being treated with the dignity he deserved, because he had been seated next to the Pope. He neglected prayer, became filled with pride, and left the community. In time, he abandoned our holy religion and ended his days in a miserable prison.

How easily we can fall. Especially when we feel lethargic in our spiritual life and begin to neglect prayer. That's why St. Josemaria wrote: "Conversion is a matter of an instant; sanctification is a task for a lifetime."

St. Alphonsus also tells the story of a famous saint who "heard in a dream a demon saying very happily: 'Whenever I bring temptations to a certain individual, I overcome and defeat him, because he does not pray asking for help.'

~181~

A few years ago, I spent several months without a job. It was a very special time for me, a spiritual spring that I fully enjoyed with my family. I dedicated more time to prayer, deepening my relationship with God, and especially getting to know Him better. In the mornings, I would wake up early and approach the window in my room. From there, I would see the wonders of creation and pray the Our Father. I started my day with excitement and hope. I remember going to see Jesus and talking to Him about it.

"Lord," I said, "since no one is hiring me, would you hire me? I would love to work for you."

After a while of silence, it seemed to me that Jesus, from that great cross, looked at me approvingly and replied, "You're hired. Now you will work for me." From that moment on, from this simple and almost childlike request, I have not had a moment of rest. I work twice as hard as I did before. Only this time, I have the best Boss. One who knows how to pay very well and never fails.

I called a friend, one of those "crazy" ones who is madly in love with Jesus, and I said, "Guess who hired me?"

"Who?" he asked curiously.

"The Lord," I replied excitedly. "The King of kings."

~182~

It is told of St. John of Kanty that one day while he was having lunch, "he saw a very hungry beggar pass by the door. He went out and gave him his lunch. He then felt such great joy upon remembering that whoever attends to the poor, attends to Christ; that afterwards, when he became a university professor, every day he gave lunch to a poor person. When someone would say to him, 'Here comes the poor man,' he would add, 'Here comes Jesus Christ.'

I always remember that night when I went for a walk with my family. In those days, I was rediscovering my faith and had many faults. As we got into the car, I saw a very poor and ragged man emerge from the darkness, walking towards me.

The first thing I felt was an unpleasant annoyance, and I prepared to say something unkind, asking him to keep moving. The man passed by me, smiled with gentle kindness, and looking me in the eyes, said: 'You have a beautiful family. They are a treasure. God bless you and bless them.' And he continued on his way without stopping.

My son Claudio Guillermo, who was 8 years old at the time, looked at me surprised and said, 'Dad, that man deserves something from you.'

'You're right,' I acknowledged, and we set out to find him. But he had disappeared. We never saw him again.

~183~

You cannot understand God's ways because His mentality is different from ours. He thinks in terms of eternity, while we think in the temporal. In God, everything is purity, love, tenderness, and we are distant from perfection. Years will pass, and one day you will realize that everything you are experiencing today was for your good.

With God, it's always like this. It's His way of teaching. Some are awakened from their sleep by His call, like Samuel. Others are thrown off their horses, like Saint Paul. And most spend the majority of their lives seeking answers, like Saint Augustine. God always reaches out to us. He has a plan for each one of us. We need to be patient and pray. Trust and have faith. If you were attentive, if you listened to His voice, every time you pray the Our Father and say, 'Father...,' you would hear Him clearly, like the wind responding, 'Child...' That's what has been happening to me with the good Lord.

~184~

"Above all, I recommend that petitions, prayers, intercessions, and thanksgivings be made for all people... This is good and pleasing to God our Savior, who wants all people to be saved and to come to a knowledge of the truth." 1 Timothy 2:1-4

Sometimes we think that God forgets us. I have come to conclude that He is always with us. He acts like a loving Father who watches over and protects His child from a distance. I know, you have made so many mistakes in your life and you can hardly pray. Do you think God has forgotten you? Do you think He doesn't love you? Open that hardened heart, be silent, just for a moment, and listen carefully:

"My child," God says to you, "Do not be afraid. I love you. You mean everything to me."

~185~

Sometimes one is left speechless and cannot pray. For me, it is enough to say: 'My Lord... and my God.' It is the best prayer I find in such moments. I leave my house, gaze at the vastness of the sky, and marvel thinking of God.

I know He is there, somewhere, watching over me. Suddenly, I am embraced by a Tenderness that surpasses all understanding. You are filled with a Love you cannot comprehend. It's like a mother's caress. You wish it would never end. It is an intense presence of God. When you find yourself without words, remember God, and you will find this brief invocation springing from your lips:

'My Lord and my God.'

At that moment, He will be present and respond to you:

'Here I am.'

~186~

To pray, you must be in the loving presence of God, attentive to His spiritual inspirations, to His Words... For this, it is beneficial to examine our inner selves, to ask ourselves a very simple question: 'Is there space for God in my life?' I suggest a very simple week during which we will sweep our soul, clean it, and prepare it like a garden to sow the Word of God. As Saint Teresa of Jesus said: 'The soul is a garden that must be cultivated.' I desire to cultivate mine and bear fruit for God.

'When one loves, one desires to speak constantly with the beloved, or at least to contemplate him incessantly. That is what prayer consists of.'

Charles de Foucauld

~187~

Has it ever happened to you? I've noticed that when I stop praying, I easily fall into temptations.

~188~

Today we will do something different, very easy and fun. Let's write down 5 things we should be grateful for. I'll share with you what I wrote.

1. Thank you, Jesus, for the life you have given me.
2. For loving me and staying with me, despite my flaws and sins.
3. For Your Mother who is our mother.
4. For the family you have granted me.
5. For my job, with which I can support them.

There is so much more to be thankful for, and I could continue filling several pages... Write your 5 reasons for gratitude. And then... let's give thanks! Let a heartfelt 'Thank you, Lord' come from your soul.

1. ____

2. ____

3. ____

4. ____

5. ____

~189~

This young woman was going through a strong emotional and spiritual crisis, feeling as though she was submerged in a dark and deep pit without finding a way out. Does this feeling of despair sound familiar to you? She remembered what her mother always told her as a child: 'When you face a problem and can't find a solution, turn to the Virgin Mary. She is your heavenly mother and will help you. The Virgin always hears our prayers and presents them to her Son, Jesus.' Desperate, she drove to a church. She needed to pray, to kneel at the feet of the Virgin, and ask her to protect her under her maternal mantle. She parked, got out of the car, and a pamphlet fell from it. She picked it up and read:

'Fifteen minutes at the feet of My Sweet Mother,
Mary Help of Christians.'

It was the answer to her prayers. It strengthened her, and she was able to move forward. I share this with you because it might help you and is very uplifting.

"My daughter, whom I tenderly love, come to my side to converse with me for a few moments; rest peacefully upon my heart and forget for a moment the sorrows of life. Look at me... I am your Mother... Can't you see in my gaze my intense and tender love? Poor daughter of mine!

Do not fear, come closer to me... No matter how great your sins are and how ungrateful you have been to me, I will not reject you; rather, I will look upon you with greater compassion... and my maternal loves, cares, and tenderness will be, my dear daughter, the means by which you will completely surrender to my Divine Son.

Tell me... what troubles you? What sorrow torments your heart the most? I can alleviate it... Why do I see you sometimes so downcast and lacking in spirit? It is because your miseries confuse you, and your constant relapses make you falter. Do not lose heart; remember that the kingdom of heaven is won through continuous effort. Think that the saints did not become saints in a moment; it is after many battles. Do not be troubled... instead of giving in to discouragement, lift your eyes to heaven and call upon me. I will come to your aid, yes... and I will heal your wounds. I will wipe away your tears, clothe you with courage, and help you to move forward. Do you know, my daughter, what is the cause of your little or no virtue and those relapses that trouble you so much? It is none other than forgetting me. If you were to invoke me frequently, you would emerge victorious in your battles and have many merits for heaven already.

You forget about me... but I have not forgotten you... and even when you do not call me, I watch over you with diligent care at all times. Who else but me has delivered you on so many occasions from the dangers that threatened you? Remember, poor daughter, your past life, and you will clearly see that, without me, you would have been prey to the infernal enemy who, furious against your soul, sought to destroy it. Recall step by step the different stages of your existence, and you will find nothing but care, love, kindness, and tender affection from the heart of your Mother who loved you before you were born. And if I watched over you even when you did not know the danger, how do you think I will abandon you now when you call upon me in the midst of your distress? No, beloved daughter, I will not leave you alone. God wants to make you a saint, but He desires from you perseverance in work and prayer. Ask much, much, my daughter... do not hesitate to ask, remember that persistent prayer penetrates the heavens and becomes a gentle dew of blessings and graces...

~190~

I had been pondering these words of Jesus for days:

'For where two or three are gathered in my name, I am there among them.' Matthew 18:20

Suddenly, I remembered this thought from Chiara Lubich: 'Jesus becomes fully present among us if we are united in His name, that is, in Him, in His will, in reciprocal love.'

And I said to myself, 'How delightful it must be to live like this. To have Jesus among us, accompanying us in every moment of the day.'

So I propose to you to live today with Jesus in the midst. To have the incredible experience of being with Him. Jesus, between you and those who offend you. In your family. In your work.

Jesus present in all your daily activities. With you and within you. Loving. Sharing. Enjoying His loving presence. You have the formula now, all you have to do is want it.

~191~

An 18-year-old reader of my books wrote to me: 'Life isn't fair. People around you abuse you, hurt you.'

It struck me to respond from the heart: 'It's true. I've experienced it. However, I have very good news for you. You can, if you choose, change this. Give your best in your work, in your home. Fill your existence with meaning. Cover everything around you with love so that others may also find love. You can be the difference, a little flame that illuminates that darkness. As Saint John of the Cross said: "Where there is no love, put love, and you will find love."

That's what I propose for this week. Live it as if it were an opportunity given to us to change the world. Let's go out ready to fill it with love. To love everyone. To love them more. To be compassionate, to be charitable, to give words of encouragement; to forget ourselves for a moment and start giving ourselves to others.

~192~

Pay attention to these words...

'The best comfort
is that which comes
from prayer.'

Saint Pio of Pietrelcina

~193~

I get the impression that you should start renewing your life by doing something extraordinary, something fulfilling that adds value to everything you do. Give it a try. Have a day of kindness, of smiling at everyone, of moving joyfully and helping wherever you can. Start the day with this prayer:

'Sweetest Lord,
You are compassionate and Merciful.'

Repeat this prayer in your mind like a short invocation. For what purpose? A very special one: 'To Gladden the Heart of God.' God likes it when we remember Him.

When you experience God and He fills you with His 'Grace' and 'Love,' you won't need anything else on this earth. Everything will lose its meaning for you except His friendship. You won't have to live trying to understand why suffering, why injustice, why all this happens to me. Knowing that God loves you and is with you will be enough. Then you can reflect God like a mirror, and others will see Him clearly in you. So much so that some will say, 'This person is of God.' Consider changing your life, turning away from sin, and pleasing GOD with your thoughts and all your actions. His grace and His love will not delay.

~194~

Once I read that God speaks to us through suffering because it is something everyone understands. Not everyone understands music, sports, or literature... but everyone knows what suffering is and understands it. That's why God chose suffering to redeem us. And that's why Jesus endured so much suffering.

Those who see the cross and Jesus on it immediately understand the message. The great saints found mystical moments contemplating the cross. You see Him nailed to that cross, suffering for you and your sins, and in that moment these words from Sacred Scripture come to your mind: 'For God so loved the world that he gave his one and only Son, that whoever believes in him shall not perish but have eternal life.' (John 3:16)

How can You love us so much, Lord? Don't You see we don't deserve it? In that moment of contemplation, you can't help but love Him. Look at Him on the Cross. Imagine that infinite pain, the torn flesh, the knees scraped from falls, the crown of thorns driven into His head. The saints, in their suffering, would say: 'It's just a small thorn compared to the many He endured with the crown of thorns.'

Forgive me, Lord, for my indifference to Your love.

~195~

Do you have many concerns? Can't find the peace you long for? Are problems overwhelming you? You ask me what you can do?

I recommend spending a day volunteering at the Home of the Missionaries of Jesus, of Mother Teresa of Calcutta. By the end of the day, you will have your answer.

This will be your 'special' activity for Saturday and Sunday. Being with the nuns, sharing what they do for the most needy, those whom no one wants to shelter.

Once, I went with a friend to deliver a donation he was making. It was a very intense and emotional moment. As we left the place, I noticed my friend was wiping his eyes with his hands. 'I don't know what's happening to me,' he said, 'I'm crying.' 'It's the grace of God,' I replied. 'He is pleased with this beautiful gesture and gifts you with that grace, an intense joy, that special emotion, that joy which is the presence of the Holy Spirit.'

I always remember that priest who had a similar experience and during Mass, in his sermon, he said, 'Do you want to be in heaven? Go where Mother Teresa's Missionaries are.' There was an emotional silence, and he confessed with excitement, 'You can feel God there.'

~196~

This morning I will take a few minutes of my life to meet with God. It will be the best moment of the day. What good is it to talk about God if we do not talk to God? What value is there in being heard if we do not listen to Him?

I will go to a solitary chapel, or to a park. And if I don't have the opportunity, I will close my eyes to imagine that I am before Him. How will my soul appear to Him? What should I do? Today we will have a wonderful activity. We will devoutly participate in Holy Mass.

This time will be different. You won't have those rushed masses or go feeling upset or agitated by daily problems. You will prepare yourself before leaving your home with a prayer. You will offer this day to God and ask Him to fill you with His grace. Then, we will go to the Church.

~197~

We are here now... The presence of God is felt. It's a small and quiet place that invites prayer. Almost every parish has a Tabernacle in a small chapel or an Oratory. Look for it and visit Jesus. If you don't see Him, ask and they will guide you. Spend some time with Jesus in that Tabernacle before Mass begins. Tell Him about this book you have brought to keep Him company, and about what you have done during the week. Talk to Him about the good things that have happened and also the adversities you are facing. He will help you, He always does. Now we must say goodbye, Mass is about to begin.

When was the last time you went to confession? A good sacramental confession would do a lot of good. Every time I confess, I tell myself, 'Listen, Jesus is going to speak to you,' because I know that Jesus also waits for me in that confessional.

Many of my friends have come out renewed after confession. I remember one who excitedly told me, 'I feel like I have been born again.'

Now pay attention to what you will hear: the readings, the Gospel, the priest's homily. Live the Mass. Experience the presence of God. We have come to the moment of consecration. How wonderful. I love looking at that white host that will soon become Jesus. When the priest elevates the consecrated host, I usually say to Him, 'Here I am, Jesus.' And He often responds, 'Here I am, Claudio.'

Before receiving communion, offer your communion for the holy souls in purgatory, for the conversion of sinners, for the well-being of your family, for the priests. There is so much to offer for. Lately, when I receive communion, I affectionately say to Jesus, 'I have you. Now you are mine.' And He curiously responds, 'I have you, Claudio. Now you are mine.'

Now return to your seat, without thinking of anything else but the Love of Loves. Leave behind the daily problems. It's a sacred moment of union between your soul and Jesus. Then, give thanks, for everything. You have your list, remember? Jesus is in you and you are in Him. What a wonderful day.

You have made the best prayer of your life. The Mass is the most complete prayer that exists, the one that pleases God the most.

As you leave the Church, enjoy Sunday, live it thinking that He is with you, therefore, you are in Him. Bring Him to others and show yourself happy, grateful. God will know how to reward you and fill you with that splendid and eternal love.

I often say, 'How good God is good,' but today it only comes from my soul to say to Him, 'Thank you, Lord.'

Have no fear.

Everything will be fine.

~198~

"In silence He listens to us; in silence He speaks to the soul and in silence we hear His voice."

Mother Teresa of Calcutta

Today will be a unique day in your life. We will be silent. We will dedicate it to God. We will set aside our mobile phones, social media, television, difficulties... and we will focus on Divine love. We will go to a chapel to pray the Rosary. Then to the oratory where the tabernacle is.

You can bring a book of spirituality to read while you accompany Jesus. These moments alone with God enrich our lives, strengthen the soul, and allow us to experience His love.

~199~

Today it happened to me again. I was at Mass and once more I thought about His silence.

"Why does it seem like you're silent?" I asked.

We reached the Our Father and I began to pray. But something interrupted me. It felt as if God was responding to me...

—Father.

—Child.

—Father.

Again:

—Child.

I smiled at this thought of His.

—Lord, I must continue. And I started again...

—Our Father

—My child.

—Who art in heaven.

—Who art on earth.

—Hallowed be thy name.

—I bless you.

—Thy kingdom come,

—I want to see all of you with me.

—Thy will be done, on earth as it is in heaven.

—It is my will that you strive, that you love, and be holy. I want you to be happy!

—Give us this day our daily bread.

—I will give you everything if you trust, love, and abandon yourself in My love.

—And forgive us our trespasses.

—I forgive and forget, again and again. That's what Love does. When you love, you can forgive thousands of times, like a Mother's heart that forgives and embraces her child.

—As we forgive those who trespass against us.

—Do you truly forgive? Think of the one who hurt you so deeply. Do you want me to help you forgive them?

—And lead us not into temptation.

—Remember, temptation is not a sin. Sometimes I allow it because it strengthens you. Sin is falling, not resisting it.

I want to ask you: What do you do when faced with great temptation? Do you pray? Do you abandon yourself to Me? Great heavenly treasures await those who persevere and triumph, those who do not succumb to temptation.

—But deliver us from evil.

—I am always with you. I care for you, comfort you, and protect you. I have a wonderful plan for each of you. In return, I ask so little. "Stay close, walk with Me, trust, obey My Commandments, be Merciful, just, holy."

You drift away from Me. You forget Me and exclude Me from your lives. You neglect the fundamental: "Love." You are like the prodigal son. My child.

I am waiting for you, with open arms, with the Love of a Father.

~200~

I know, you don't have to tell me. I sensed it. As you read this, you feel like you're standing on the edge of a cliff and you don't know how you got there, why you feel this way. You have no energy to pray or approach the sacraments. The world has struck you too hard, and you think you can't go on, that you're not loved, that you've reached the end of the road. You are not alone, nor are you the only one feeling this way.

How cunning the devil is. He knows our weaknesses. He knows that if he corners us, we will neglect what strengthens us: prayer, the sacraments.

I have known many people like you, who have faced immense difficulties, great sufferings, heartbreaks, abandonments, injustices, and in the end, lost everything. I have always been impressed by how they managed to move forward, victorious, renewed, strengthened. They never gave up. They regained everything lost and multiplied it. Is it possible? Yes, I have seen it. I heard of this enterprising woman who lost her business and ended up in ruin.

She spoke with a priest friend who advised her, "In everything you do, keep God in mind." She followed the advice and started anew.

Suddenly, her business improved, and she recovered her fortune. This time, with the joy of a purpose: "to serve others." She is happier than ever. She shares 10% of her profits with her employees, makes significant donations, and her company is a stable and dignified source of employment for many.

Though it may seem impossible, there is a way out, a path to discover. God always gives you new opportunities.

~201~

"To pray with unlimited hope of being heard."
Saint John Bosco

Pray, even when you feel you can't go on. Pray, even when the world is crashing down on you. Pray, even when everyone has turned their back on you. Pray, even when you see no solution to your problems. Pray, even when you believe you are not being heard.

Persist in your prayer.

God always listens and prayer strengthens you.

~202~

There is so much that a woman of good habits can do with her example, often without realizing it. Due to her husband's work, my sister-in-law Alma moved to a picturesque village in Mexico. Everyone there was cordial, kind, cheerful, and filled with beautiful traditions. But there was a badly behaved boy who was everyone's nightmare, and no one knew what to do with him.

Every morning, Alma would walk to a nearby town for the 6:00 a.m. mass. The boy became curious about this daily walk and one morning he stopped her.

"Where do you go every morning that you come back so radiant and happy?" "To mass." "Can I come with you?" "If your mother gives you permission."

The next morning, the boy awaited her on the road, dressed in his best clothes, with permission from his mother, and he accompanied her to mass. From then on, he went daily. When my sister-in-law left the village to move to another town with her family, that once troublesome boy had become an example to all, well-behaved and without foul language. He ended up becoming the altar boy for the village, assisting the good priest during mass.

~203~

"Humble yourselves, therefore, under the mighty hand of God, so that at the proper time he may exalt you. Cast all your anxieties on him, because he cares for you."
1 Peter 5:6-7

I bear a Biblical message that I must deliver to you. It's no longer a whisper. "God loves you and cares for you."

Be happy! Don't be afraid. Persevere! Fight! Come on, you can do it! Don't give up! Don't be discouraged!

Cast your worries upon God. He is our Father and he cares for you.

~204~

There are two prayers taught by the Angel in Fatima to the little shepherds that serve to intercede before God for sinners.

1. **First Prayer:** "My God, I believe, I adore, I hope, and I love You! I ask pardon for those who do not believe, do not adore, do not hope, and do not love You!" (Three times).
2. **Second Prayer:** "Most Holy Trinity, Father, Son, and Holy Spirit, I adore You profoundly and I offer You the Most Precious Body, Blood, Soul, and Divinity of Our Lord Jesus Christ, present in all the tabernacles of the world, in reparation for the outrages by which He is offended. By the infinite merits of the Sacred Heart of Jesus and the Immaculate Heart of Mary, I beg the conversion of sinners."

The second time the Angel appeared to the children, he found them playing and asked, "What are you doing?" He then urged them, "Pray, pray a great deal; offer prayers and sacrifices to the Most High." Lucia, confused by these words, dared to ask, "But how are we to sacrifice ourselves?" The Angel replied:

"In every way you can, offer a sacrifice to God to atone for the sins by which He is offended...

~205~

This morning I sat down to pray on the bed. I have so many questions. I have come to the conclusion that sometimes our only mission is to sow the seed of love in someone's heart. How to do it? It's not that difficult. It's like plowing the field. Open the furrow to plant the seed.

The heart is complicated. It is worked on through love and prayer. You must love and pray, so you will know when it is ready. At that moment, you will sow that little seed. The rest, God will take care of. He is the one who makes it germinate and grow into a bush or a leafy tree. After pondering this, I read this beautiful prayer: 'Make me water for your fields. Light for your seeds. Servant who cleans your stable. Mouth that repeats your words. Ears that hear your children. Legs that conquer distances. Heart that extends to hearts. Accompany me, Lord, and never leave me.'

I am tired of walking and searching, without finding anything. I prefer to surrender in your love. May my hands be your hands, my feet yours. I will extend the sails of my soul, so that you, Lord, may blow and take me wherever you want.

At that moment, a sweet voice reached my heart: 'Trust, surrender, God will do it well.'

~206~

My cousin Gabriel has his house on the outskirts of San José, Costa Rica. It used to be a farm, and he has turned it into a wonderful place.

His wife has just overcome cancer. With her immune system weakened, she couldn't be in crowds and they missed attending Mass. They began to pray.

Days later, the priest from the area called them, asking if they could celebrate Mass at their home for the neighbors.

It was incredible! Now, every Sunday they start the day with Holy Mass.

~207~

Once I read about a sick child who went to the sanctuary of Lourdes. The Blessed Sacrament passed by his stretcher in procession, but nothing happened. When the priest returned and passed by again, the child shouted, "Jesus, if you don't heal me, I will tell your Mother." Instantly, he was healed.

The miracles associated with the apparitions of the Virgin at Lourdes are profound and capable of dispelling any skepticism. Let me share a chilling story that happened some years ago...

Some young people decided to expose what they considered "the church's fraud" and wanted to mock the Blessed Sacrament and the apparitions at Lourdes. To do this, they traveled to France and hired a man blind from birth to assist them.

Their plan was to create a disturbance when the Blessed Sacrament passed by. On the appointed day, they carried out their plan. The priest passed by and made the sign of the cross with the Blessed Sacrament in front of them. But before they could mock or protest, the blind man surprised them. Something unexpected had happened! The previously blind man started jumping, waving his hands, and covering his eyes while shouting excitedly, "I can see! It's a miracle! I can see!" The young people scattered in fear, unable to comprehend what had just occurred.

Years passed. One of them married a devout woman who taught catechism to a group of children on Saturday mornings. The husband became curious about his wife's activities and decided to spy on her one morning. He followed her to the church and hid behind a column.

Meanwhile, his wife gathered the children in the inner courtyard where there is a replica of the Lourdes grotto. They began to pray with great tenderness. Soon after, they sang to the Virgin with such purity and affection that he was deeply moved and began to cry.

That same day, he went to confession and regained his inner peace. His wife was amazed. The next day, he participated devoutly in Holy Mass and received Communion. After Mass, he approached the priest, shook his hands firmly, and said with conviction, "The Virgin has saved me!"

~208~

"Give it a try and you will see how good the Lord is."
Psalm 34

Do not be afraid. I know hundreds of cases of people who have learned to trust. Their lives have changed because God has shown Himself in their midst. They asked, and God granted them beyond what they once dreamed. These are small miracles that happen every day. Just trust and love, and let God act in our lives, accepting His holy will like a woman of faith, which is perfect and for our well-being. See in everything the powerful and fatherly hand of God at work.

~209~

"Before I formed you in the womb I knew you, before you were born I set you apart..." Jeremiah 1:5

Everything will turn out well. Trust and walk according to God's will. He is the one who organizes your life. Do what He asks and go where He sends you. Let Him inspire your life. Let no one or nothing distract you from God. A woman of faith walks according to God's will. She accepts everything, offers everything. Your life and your heart should remain at all times under His sweet protection.

~210~

THOUGHTS

- Do you suffer frequent temptations? Learn from the saints: consecrate yourself to the Virgin Mary. She will protect you.
- Whoever knows Jesus can only love Him.
- People despair because they do not know God.
- I like Jesus' words to the Samaritan woman: "If you knew the gift of God and who it is that asks you for a drink, you would have asked him and he would have given you living water."
- What we lack is tenderness. The innocence of a child. Trust in the Father. Knowing Jesus.
- If we pay a little attention, we can know God's designs.
- The pain of a simple sin (can there be such a thing as a simple sin?) is such that it urges us to reconciliation.
- Peace in the heart comes from forgiveness. That's why we must forgive and be forgiven.
- Forgive those who have offended us and approach the confessional to receive God's forgiveness.
- Start making spiritual communions. Afterwards, everything will be sweetness, tenderness, and joy. It's like being on a cloud outside of this world.

~211~

When I feel sad, I think of God.
When I feel lonely, I think of God.
When I feel exhausted, I think of God.
When I find myself at a crossroads, I think of God.
When I suffer, I think of God.
When I feel my strength is not enough, I think of God.

Then, everything becomes clear. The gloomy outlook turns into a summer evening. Sunny. Beautiful. Because God is my Father. And I know with certainty that He does everything for my good. It is holy abandonment. Complete trust. Knowing that, with Him, we can do all things. God wants you for Himself, pure of heart.

~212~

"Truly I tell you, if you have faith the size of a mustard seed, you will say to this mountain, 'Move from here to there,' and it will move. Nothing will be impossible for you." Matthew 17:20

God does not resist a soul that is in love and trusts. Everything would be possible for you if only you trusted a little more. I have seen it countless times. I have seen God pass by and touch people. I have seen how He has transformed them. I have witnessed the miracles that God has performed in so many people. If only you loved Him a little more. Do not be afraid, little sheep of God. Do not fear. Nothing bad will happen. Everything will be for your good. It will always be the best. With God, the best is always yet to come.

You ask God with fear about the future. You ask God without the certainty that faith brings. You say to me, "I pray, I go to Mass, I ask God, and nothing happens. How should I pray, Claudio?" It's better that Jesus answers you. Open your Bible and let's hear what He says: "Have faith in God. Truly I tell you, if anyone says to this mountain, 'Go, throw yourself into the sea,' and does not doubt in their heart but believes that what they say will happen, it will be done for them. Therefore I tell you, whatever you ask for in prayer, believe that you have received it, and it will be yours." (Mark 11:22-24)

Now you know. It's not enough to ask and pray. You must have faith, trust that you will receive. Love God with all your heart and soul. You must: — Love. — Seek God out of love. — Be a Woman with a faith that withstands everything. — Live in His loving presence.

You will discover in that moment that whatever happens, no matter how bad it may seem, will always be the best, because God has allowed it for your good.

In a dream I heard clearly: "If you feel attacked, pray the Hail Mary." So, asleep, I obeyed. And the storm passed.

~213~

I must unfurl the sails of my soul. It's not where I want to go, but where You want me to go, Lord.

I just watch, wait, trust. And when I reach the harbor, I ask You: "What do You want from me, Lord?"

~214~

A few months ago, I was in Costa Rica visiting family. My sister-in-law Susana took me to the "San José" Church in Heredia. The priest, in his homily, said some words that I loved and wrote down:

"The Christian is a person of hope. They are not a defeated person. Behind every event, the Christian seeks the hand of God. That's why they are a person of hope. We must have discernment, asking why this has happened. What is the purpose? What does God want from me?"

In the face of pain, you must surrender yourself into the hands of God, without doubting, without fearing. Trusting. Serene.

Beloved Jesus, if people truly knew you, they would have no fears, nor worry about the future, because you are the best of friends. Noble. Sincere. Good. And you love us all, no matter how much we have offended you, without seeing our sins. You see the best in us. What we could become if only we trusted a little more.

~215~

"... why do you wish to avoid the cross, by which you will enter the kingdom? In the cross is health, in the cross is life, in the cross is the protection against enemies, in the cross is the infusion of sovereign sweetness, in the cross is the strength of the heart, in the cross is the joy of the spirit, in the cross is the highest virtue, in the cross is the perfection of holiness. There is no salvation for the soul, nor hope of eternal life, except in the cross. Take up, therefore, your cross, and follow Jesus, and you will go to eternal life." (Imitation of Christ / Kempis)

Some people think that because I write these books on spiritual growth, I do not face difficulties, that life has been kind to me. Difficulties? I have them, like everyone else. No one is exempt from suffering. But I move forward. Every time I stumble, I tell myself: "Trust, Claudio. You must trust." I follow the advice of Saint Teresa of Jesus: "Embrace your cross, it is easier to bear." I accept it and embrace it, even though I may not like it, because I know it is what God expects of me, to accept His will and embrace my cross. I write these words of encouragement on the palm of my hand, like a child embracing his Father: "Do not be afraid. I am with you."

~216~

Cultivate temperance.

It is the fourth theological virtue. How will it help you? "It helps you weigh and measure your words carefully. It encourages thoughtful speech. It prevents a moment of anger from ruining relationships and friendships that can only be rebuilt with difficulty later on."

~217~

"Love the Lord your God with all your heart, with all your soul, and with all your mind." Matthew 22:37

"Whoever does not love God binds their heart to things that pass like smoke. The more one knows people, the less one loves them. With God it is the opposite: the more one knows Him, the more one loves Him. This knowledge sets the soul on fire with such love that those who know Him only love and desire God. Love for God is a foretaste of heaven: if we knew how to taste it, how happy we would be. What makes us unhappy is not loving God!"

Saint John Vianney

~218~

I really liked this reflection by Chiara Lubich, the founder of the Catholic Movement of the Focolare, so I'm sharing it with you:

Seeing Jesus in our neighbor.

"We can love Jesus also in our family members to whom we say good morning, with whom we might pray in the morning or have breakfast.

We can love Jesus in our neighbors throughout the day, even behind the school desk where we teach, or at the counter of a business, or at the bank teller where we work...

We can love our neighbor by seeing Jesus in them at home, when we sweep or mop the floor, when we wash the dishes or go shopping.

We always have this wonderful opportunity, and we can be sure that on each occasion He says to us: 'You did it to me.'

~219~

Has it happened to you? The storm came. Suddenly I found myself immersed in a big problem. A friend, seeing me worried, said these comforting words: "Cheer up Claudio. It's just a stone in your shoe." It gave me the feeling that it's something we can fix. You take off your shoe, shake it out, and you're good to go! After our conversation, I sat down to think and realized that many people have this annoying stone in their shoe. We confront so many problems. What to do? I decided to move forward, to persevere. I wasn't going to give up; I would be perseverant, I would trust in God. My life is like a boat, I unfurl the sails of my soul and let God blow and His wind take me wherever He wants. You see, when it comes to suffering, we can row in the same boat, because suffering is for everyone, just like God's love is for everyone. Suffering often motivates us to see the world from another perspective, one that is more humane, understanding, full of mercy. Through suffering, we can understand those who suffer, ally with them, embrace them, console them. There is a reason for everything in life. If you suffer, offer it up. The world needs your offerings, your prayers, and your penances. Don't forget the awe-inspiring words of the Virgin at Lourdes to Saint Bernadette: "Penance, penance, penance! Pray to God for sinners." Suffering can help so many souls if you offer it, if you embrace the cross that the good Lord has placed on your shoulders. You turn pain into a spiritual treasure. In the end, everything will pass. It always does. Come on! Don't worry about anything. Everything will be fine. Cheer up!

~220~

Life is not simple, often it's not fair, but it's wonderful, worth it. It's a grace, a gift from God. Life is meant to be lived. Don't waste it complaining about what could have been, suffering unnecessarily. At my age, I've understood this. The most valuable thing you possess isn't your houses, cars, or savings. It's not even something you own or can sell. It's time. Your time in life. And you must make the most of it. Don't waste it. I'm sure right now you have that problem spinning in your head that you don't know how to solve, right? You try to get it out of your mind and it always comes back, like a boomerang. It hits you. It fills you with worries. First, it fills you with fears and anxieties. "What will I do?" you ask yourself, but the answer is not near. You talk to friends and tell them, hoping someone will give you words of encouragement. It's terrible to live like this, with that anguish. You're not living and you're losing valuable moments that will never come back.

You have to pause. Stop the path and explore all your options. I know from experience that this will pass. I've seen it hundreds of times. Everything passes. This too. Relax.

~221~

While writing the reflection for this wonderful day, I received a phone call. It was from a lady who was suffering and didn't know what to hold on to. For some reason, I felt compelled to say to her:

"I'll tell you the words that pour out from my heart. Words for you and your family. Don't be afraid, God walks with you, in your joys and your pain. He has always been with you."

I gave her the recommendation I give to everyone, the best thing I can say, something I've proven, not just a theory: "Go visit Jesus in the Tabernacle. He has the answers you're looking for." Everyone I tell to visit Jesus experiences something spectacular. They return transformed, eager to tell me about their great adventures rediscovering God.

A good confession helps a lot. And more, participating in Holy Mass and receiving communion devoutly. If we fill ourselves with God, life will be bearable, joyful, sweet. With God, the best is always yet to come.

~222~

How does your soul awaken today?

~223~

I'll tell you something from my life, for its lesson. On Sundays, I used to set up a small table with my books in one of the corridors of the National Shrine of the Heart of Mary. Often, I would sit there waiting between Masses, wondering to myself, "What am I doing here?" I wait. I reflect. And I pray. I would rather be with Vida, my wife, taking a walk with my children. But something very intimate, deep, tells me that I must stay there for that moment, that it is what God wants from me, that my sacrifice pleases Him.

One afternoon, an acquaintance attended the 6:00 PM Mass and glanced at me as he passed by. He avoided me. I sensed in his look a hint of displeasure, a subtle message: "Poor Claudio, look at where he's ended up." I felt ashamed that he saw me in those circumstances. God always comes to our aid, like a good Father. At that moment, I remembered a scene from the life of St. Francis of Assisi. He had just forsaken all comforts to follow God and went from door to door begging alms for his poor. On one occasion, he encountered his friends joyfully celebrating, eating and drinking. Francis hesitated, felt ashamed, but gathered his courage and entered, surprising his friends, asking for alms. That gesture gave me strength. I asked God for forgiveness and said to myself, "Why should I be ashamed of what God asks of me?"

I must be humble and ask God for that grace, which is so difficult to conquer.

One doesn't know God's reasons. I only know that I've witnessed miracles around that simple book stand. People reconciling, a young woman choosing not to abort, others deciding to forgive, some renewing their lives, and others deciding for God.

I used to have university students with me who helped. The first is now a doctor. The other lost his way for a time. One afternoon, he returned wearing a Franciscan habit. I stood up in surprise. It was amazing! I gave him a long hug and asked for his blessing.

I listened to many people who stopped and shared their lives with me for some reason, and I marveled at how kind God is to them.

One day I was tired, annoyed, wondering if it was worth being there, offering my books. Wasn't it better to look for sales points instead? Just then, a lady came out of the chapel where the Blessed Sacrament is kept, walked past me, stopped, and said, "Do not be troubled. It's worth it, what you're doing, it's worth it." She pointed to the Blessed Sacrament, "And He is pleased to see you here." And then she walked away. She left me stunned. It was incredible! Since then, I went happily with my little table and my books, thinking that if God wanted it, so did I.

~224~

To uplift myself, I have a large sign in my room at home that says:

"WITH GOD,
THE BEST
IS YET TO COME."

~225~

Sometimes, I don't know why, but a boundless tenderness wells up from my soul, as if God Himself were present and enveloping me in His Love. I haven't always fully understood these events, I just know they happen, and they lead me to do curious things.

One day, I remembered that despite being so close, I visited Him infrequently. So, at times, I would close my eyes and, in my mind, I would transport myself to the chapel to keep Him company. It's so comforting to be in His presence... When I think of Jesus, it moves me to action. Today, for example, I stayed awake until midnight to write to you and share my experiences. At this hour, everyone at home is asleep, and I can think, pray, reflect... I even feel like giving Him a new name. I call Him "Tenderness," what a whimsical thought of mine. What pleases me most is when you experience His closeness... you know it's Him and He is near. An inexplicable love overwhelms you... We love Him more than ever and we tell Him so. Then it seems to me that I see Him smiling with so much joy in that sanctuary, and with so much love that everything is light, serenity, and peace. And that's when you hear His sweet words in your soul:

"I love you too."

~226~

Every night after finishing her night shift, Teresa walked alone through the park to reach the other side where her house was. This shortcut saved her half an hour of walking. That night, a strange man stopped her. He emerged from the bushes, wielding a sharp knife. He looked at her with lust and deep hatred. Terrified, she closed her eyes and prayed that ancient prayer our grandmothers taught us:

"Angel of my guard, my sweet company,
do not forsake me, neither night nor day..."

She heard a noise, opened her eyes, and saw the man fleeing in fear. The next day, the newspapers reported a girl murdered at that hour in the same park. "It's not a coincidence," she thought, and went to the police. She recounted her experience in detail and described the man, from which they created a composite sketch. They captured him days later lurking around the park. She requested to speak with him, which they allowed, and this dialogue took place:

—Do you remember me?
—I remember you well.
—Were you going to harm me?
—Yes.

—What stopped you? Why did you run away?
—The strange man stopped me.
—What man? I was alone.

—You wasn't alone. By your side, protecting you, appeared a huge man, blond-haired, muscular, dressed in luminous clothing like I had never seen. I got scared and ran away.

There are some phrases by Saint Josemaría Escrivá about the Guardian Angel that I really like: "Have confidence in your Guardian Angel. Treat him like an intimate friend —which he is— and he will do you a thousand favors in the ordinary affairs of each day."

He also said: "When I go to one of our oratories where the tabernacle is, I say to Jesus that I love Him, and I invoke the Trinity. Then I give thanks to the Angels who guard the Tabernacle, adoring Christ in the Eucharist."

The Catechism of the Church tells us: "No one can deny the fact that each faithful has beside him an angel as protector and shepherd leading him to life."

Teach your children, nephews, grandchildren from a young age to interact with their Guardian Angel. It will bring them great favors in their lives.

~227~

Nothing bad can happen,
if God is with you.

~228~

If one day Jesus were to ask me:
"What do you want, Claudio?
What can I give you?"

I would answer without hesitation:
"I want you, good Jesus, because having you,
I have everything."

And you, what would you answer?

~229~

At my age, life takes on different meanings. I have seen my children born, I have seen my father depart, I have read many books and written others. I have planted trees. And at times, I have felt the living presence of God in my small heart. Every time I approach communion, I look at Jesus in those white, beautiful, consecrated hosts, and I tell Jesus a thousand times that I love him, that I am happy knowing he is my friend. His friendship has accompanied me throughout my days. I know he is with me, as he is with you. As a child, my greatest desire was to be holy, to please Jesus. I remember a sweet nun to whom I confessed, and she asked me, "And now?" "Now even more," I replied. "But I make so many mistakes..."

We live by grace, sustained by the infinite Love of the Father. I realize how small we are and how great God is. And I love knowing that I am his child, that we are his children and, therefore, siblings. I have always felt that this search for God is like climbing a mountain. I often roll downhill, but I persist and start climbing again. And as I climb, I think: "I must strive, love more. I will love those who hurt me, those who do not understand me, those who love me." Life is so short that it is worth spending it on something greater than ourselves, on someone: "God."

Life is meant to be lived. We have come into this world to be happy, to love.

~230~

"Everything works for the good of those who love God."
Romans 8:28

Surely you've noticed it already. You go to Mass, you pray the Rosary, you visit the Blessed Sacrament, and you perform acts of charity, but everything remains the same. Nothing changes. Where is that peace that God promised you? Why do you feel worse despite everything you do?

You're missing something fundamental abandoning yourself in the loving hands of God, looking to Jesus and trusting like a woman of faith in the Divine will.

We learn this from the testimony given by the saints. Saint Thomas More, before he died, wrote a letter of comfort to his daughter in which he affirmed:

"Nothing can happen to me that God does not will. And everything that He wills, no matter how bad it may seem to us, is actually the best."

You must give your faith the seasoning that gives flavor to the soup. It's called trust. You must trust in God. Have the certainty that everything that happens to you, however terrible it may seem, will be the best for you because God has allowed it. And God, who is good, will never allow something to happen to you that is not for the benefit of your soul and your eternity.

I remind you of this passage from the Bible. Read it carefully and you will find the answers to your concerns (Matthew 14): "Peter said to Him in reply, 'Lord, if it is You, command me to come to You on the water.' He said, 'Come.' Peter got out of the boat and began to walk on the water toward Jesus. But when he saw how [strong] the wind was he became frightened; and, beginning to sink, he cried out, 'Lord, save me!' Immediately Jesus stretched out His hand and caught him, and said to him, 'O you of little faith, why did you doubt?'"

Did you notice? For those few seconds Peter trusted, he walked on the water in the midst of that storm. Do you know what this is? An extraordinary miracle. And he only had to trust, forget his fears, and look at Jesus. When he became distracted and stopped looking at Jesus, he succumbed to his fears. The key is to look at Jesus, not ourselves.

A friend who is a Franciscan friar once told me: "If you look at Jesus, you will see great wonders, a God for whom nothing is impossible. If you look at yourself, you will only see your fears, your sins, and your miseries."

The key is to look at Jesus, not ourselves, to have faith, and to believe in His Word.

~231~

I came to see Jesus because of a very serious problem. And I didn't know how to solve it. When you go through a very difficult situation, you often look up to heaven and seek God. I took advantage that Mass had not yet begun and entered to chat with Him in this beautiful oratory, where everything is peace and serenity. In this silence, I realized that I came to ask for favors, not to tell Him that I loved Him. It wasn't right to visit Him out of convenience. I wanted to see Him because I miss Him, because I love feeling His loving presence, and I prayed with all my heart:

Draw me near to You, Lord, out of love. Not because I suffer. Or because of a problem. Or because this anguish eats away at my soul. Or out of need. Or a favor. Or an illness.

May I seek You because I love You. Because You are my friend. Teach me to trust, to place my problems in Your hands. May I love, to truly love You, as You deserve, with a pure and selfless love. This is the grace I ask of You."

Then something unexpected, surprising happened. I felt a sweet inner voice comforting me: "Do not be afraid," it said to me, "I am with you." The Mass began. In the middle of the homily, I remembered those words and wrote them on the palm of my hand to keep them with me all day. "Do not be afraid. I am with you." As I finished writing them, I looked up and the priest said, "Do not be afraid," God tells you. "He is with you." I looked at him surprised and he continued: "There cannot be a Christian without a cross. But that heavy cross, we cannot bear it alone. Ask Jesus to help you and your cross will be light and bearable." It was amazing. How much peace I experienced in that moment. I regained serenity. The certainty of knowing that Jesus was with me. So I made an important decision: "Between uncertainty and trust, I choose to trust. I will trust despite everything. May Your holy will be done in me, Lord." That act of surrender made a big difference. I left Mass calm, happy. The problems were resolved. And best of all, it happened today because I came to see Jesus, out of love.

~232~

Once I went to a Catholic radio station to talk about Jesus.

"Give me the opportunity," I told the station's director. "I recently visited Jesus in a chapel; now I need to speak about Him."

"I don't know why," she replied, "but I believe it will be worthwhile."

The program lasted an hour, and we received countless calls. We talked about our little books and how Jesus was transforming hearts around us. We were very surprised. Jesus certainly knows how to do things well. Sometimes he likes surprises, and the best was saved for last.

When we left the studio with the station manager, we saw a taxi suddenly pull up outside. The driver hurriedly got out and flung open the station's door, nearly knocking it down. He stood before us. I didn't know what was happening. Suddenly, this man accustomed to the tough life of the streets began to cry.

He looked at us, distressed, and apologized, "I can't help it," he said between sobs. "It's the emotion. God loves me!"

I hugged him warmly, and we sat on a bench.

"Don't worry," I told him, "I also cry when Jesus passes by. That's just how He is."

He then told me that it was his birthday that day, that he had asked Jesus for a favor, and that he found his answer on this radio program. I stopped seeing him as a stranger and felt him as a brother. And I believe he will be one since then.

"How great You are, Lord," I said to myself, surprised to see the wonders He works with His own.

~233~

When you restore grace in your soul, God becomes present and you begin to experience small everyday miracles, each better than the last. It's something astonishing. I often tell people, "You must have the experience of God. Only then will you lose your fears." Because, if you have the experience, you will realize that you are not alone, that God is your Father, and that He truly loves you. Words will never penetrate as deeply as experience. Being in God's hands. Living immersed in His Love. Knowing yourself as His daughter. Having that certainty is what will truly change your life.

Today, I spoke with a friend who is living through these experiences. Her life has undergone a radical change. She tells me stories that leave me impressed. Yesterday, for instance, she was driving her car and felt the need to stop at a Church she rarely attends because it's far from her home. She didn't understand why, but she parked in front of the Church. It was like a calling. She got out of the car and went into the oratory, to a side where there is a beautiful painting of the Virgin Mary. There she saw a very humble young girl, about fourteen years old, speaking to the Virgin, pouring out her troubles. My friend was struck by the innocence and familiarity with which the girl spoke to the Virgin. She called her aside and said, "You know, I have a message for you. You are very special. The Virgin loves you with crazy passion and madness." And she gave her a five-dollar bill. "This is for you to come back whenever you want."

The young girl started crying. She hugged my friend very emotionally. "I will never forget what you've told me. I will keep it in my heart for my whole life. To get here, I took four buses and didn't have a single cent to return home."

At that moment, my friend understood. And she thanked the Virgin for allowing her to be a small instrument of her love.

~234~

A friend told me long ago:

"It's not the same to talk about God, as it is to experience God. You must feel His presence, live His love."

I realized he was right. God gives you a treasure that many seek in the wrong places. He makes you happy. He doesn't take away your problems, but He makes you happy. He strengthens you, fills you with peace and serenity. Now I live my life as I always wanted, in the presence of God. I write, enjoy my family, and learn to see creation as a great Gift entrusted to us.

Every morning I wake up and my first words are: "Thank you, Lord." Why? ... As Saint Clare of Assisi said, "for having created me," and I continue: "for life, for being my Father, for my family, for faith, for your Son, for creation."

Then I go outside and sit down. I close my eyes and listen to the birds.

What a wonder!

"Thank you, Lord."

~235~

One morning, I left for work late. I was speeding to arrive early. On a small street, I found a truck moving very slowly. It was driven by an elderly man with his young granddaughter. Sometimes the girl looked back and waved at me. I smiled and waved back.

I needed to pass them. As I prepared to do so, I felt a voice telling me, "Pray for them." I slowed down instead of overtaking them, and I prayed, "Lord, protect them." In that split second, another car sped out of the intersection, lost control on the curve, and crashed head-on into them. It was a loud, violent collision.

I got out of my car and rushed to help them. Neighbors also came out to assist. It was shocking; their car was destroyed, but they emerged unharmed. The driver who caused the accident was a young man who was drunk.

A woman touched my shoulder. I turned around, and she said, "God loves you very much." "Why do you say that?" "I was outside my house and saw you about to pass the car that got hit. Suddenly, you stopped and didn't. That crash was meant for you. What happened?" "I prayed," I replied. "I stopped to pray for them. By doing that, they were saved, and I was saved too. Prayer saved us all."

~236~

Years ago, a group of young people from the Focolare Catholic group had a serious accident. Their car went off a cliff, and they were all scattered at the bottom of the ravine. They were severely injured and could barely move. Suddenly, one of them, very weakly, whispered:

"God is Love."

And the others, as best they could, repeated this phrase: "God is Love." That's how they passed away one after another, with the sweet name of God on their lips.

~237~

God knows how to bring good out of what seems misfortune to us. It's like the gardener who prunes a tree to strengthen it. Perhaps at this moment, God is pruning the tree of your life. It's painful but necessary. In time, you will see it.

A few days ago, a friend sent me a desperate message online. We were communicating on a platform where people can chat in real time. Distressed, he said:

"I've reached the end of the road." "I don't understand." "This afternoon, the bank is going to foreclose on my house. They'll take everything I have." "God tests your little faith to teach you to trust. You must find Him even in the storms," I said calmly. And I added: "Nothing will happen." "What you're saying is impossible." "Everything is possible for God."

I advised him as I always do in such cases: "Visit Jesus in the Blessed Sacrament, tell Him everything. He will know what to do." "Will God listen to me?" "He always does. You'll see."

Then he apologized: "Give me a minute, someone's calling me on my phone."

I waited...

Later, he wrote excitedly: "I can't believe it! This is incredible. While I was still talking to you, a friend called me offering the money I need." "If you trust," I told him, "you will see even greater things."

And I thought gratefully: "How good you are, Lord."

~238~

"To be joyful is prayer, a sign of our generosity, of our detachment and of our inner union with God."

Mother Teresa of Calcutta

Be happy, joyful. Don't let anything or anyone take away the joy of living.

~239~

"Therefore, I will allure her,
I will lead her into the desert
and speak tenderly to her."
Hosea 2:16

If you open your heart, you will hear Him in the gentle breeze, because God speaks to the heart of man. To do so, you must empty your heart. Only what is empty can be filled. Souls of prayer are souls of profound silence. We must hear God in the depths of the heart and in His Word.

Saint Ambrose said:

"When we pray, we speak with God. And when we read the divine words, we listen to Him."

I always remember the time I went to Mass and said to Jesus, "Never leave me." At the end of Mass, I noticed there was a Bible open on the side of the altar. I approached with curiosity and read amazed: "I will never leave you nor forsake you." (Hebrews 13:5)

~240~

THE TAXI DRIVER OF GOD

Of all the stories I've published, this one has impressed readers the most. I collected it in my book, "The Great Secret." Every time I go on a radio station, they ask me to tell it. And the effects are astonishing. I usually include it in my books because of how uplifting it is.

God has unexpected surprises for us along the way. He always accompanies us and watches over us.

My mom experienced it two days ago.

She was in a supermarket and started feeling a bit unwell. She went outside to find a taxi to take her home and found a huge line of people also waiting for one. Then... (Let's hear it from her.)

"I said to God, 'Send me a taxi that belongs to You.'

Just then, a taxi at the back drove straight past the crowd and stopped in front of me.

'Where are you going?' the taxi driver asked, rolling down the window.

'To El Carmen neighborhood.'

'Come on, get in. I'll take you.'

'Sir,' I said, 'you are very fortunate because you are a man of God. Your taxi belongs to God. I just asked God to send me one of His taxis, and suddenly you arrived.'

The taxi driver looked at me, impressed.

'Madam,' he said, 'I don't know why, but I felt the urge to move forward. I didn't pick up anyone who was before you. I came straight to you.' Then he smiled.

'Look at what it says on the door,' he said excitedly.

Next to me, on the door, there was a large sign that said:

THIS TAXI, IS FROM GOD.

~241~

Imagine your life is difficult—whose life is simple? The Cross accompanies us. Problems abound, temptations are plentiful. We live amidst so many struggles... Yet, our good God has understood you well, which is why He compensates your efforts by giving you the "graces" you need to keep going. It's so easy to fall into sin, to live submerged in it. The world makes it easy for us to offend God, who is so good and loves us so much.

You suddenly discover that you're stuck in the mud. You don't know how to get out of it. Every day you think about what to do and can't decide. Saint Paul himself wrote: "I do not understand my own actions. For I do not do what I want, but I do the very thing I hate... I can will what is right, but I cannot do it. For I do not do the good I want, but the evil I do not want is what I do" (Romans 7:15-19). Often temptation comes to us as a soft and sweet voice. These are thoughts that seem pleasant. They seduce you. Deep down, you know it's not right, but your flesh overcomes you and you fall. Do you know what we lack? Prayer. We are weak. We are men and women of clay, who pray little.

Saint Josemaria Escriva wrote these warnings for you and me: "Do not dialogue with temptation. Let me repeat it: have the courage to flee; and the strength to not toy with your weakness, thinking about how far you could go. Cut it off without concessions!"

"We must foster in our souls a true horror of sin. Lord—say it again with a contrite heart—let me not offend you anymore!"

"You flirt with temptations, you put yourself in danger, you play with sight, imagination..."

This morning, I opened my Bible seeking an answer to these questions. It was surprising. God speaks to us in so many wonderful ways. This one was so clear and direct, piercing to the deepest parts of the heart: "Awake, O sleeper, and arise from the dead, and Christ will shine on you." (Ephesians 5:14) If you die in mortal sin, you will have lost a brilliant eternity beside God. Your life will have been in vain.

Recently, you asked me: "Is there hope for me? I've been away from God for years."
— Yes, there is hope, because God has loved you from all eternity.

It's as if God Himself were asking you:
— Which is greater, your sin or my Mercy?
— Your Mercy, Lord.
— Then why do you doubt?

~242~

God has placed many signs in the world for us to see and understand His will, the path we should follow. Throughout my life, I have discovered many of them. The one that impresses me the most is the cross.

The saints tell us that the Cross is the sure path to Paradise, and Saint Rose of Lima clarified: "Outside of the Cross there is no other ladder by which we may get to Heaven." To suffer with patience is to die to oneself in order to live in God. Offering our sufferings is carrying our cross out of love for Jesus. We suffer and at the same time we are filled with graces in the presence of God.

Thomas à Kempis wrote in his "The Imitation of Christ": "Be assured, it is profitable to die to oneself, to live to God; and that you must willingly suffer a little, to gain eternal life; as also to let go all temporal things, for the gaining of the kingdom of heaven."

~243~

Did you know that in the Bible there are more than 3,500 promises of God for humanity? The problem is that we often cannot access them because we either do not know them or do not believe God. One of the most important to me is found in Matthew 28:20:

"I am with you always, even to the end of the age."

Our lives would be much better if we believed God. He has made so many promises to us. Have you ever read them? Do you know what He has promised you?

First, that He will never abandon you.

Second, that you will always have His unconditional love.

And third, that if you trust in Him, all things will be possible.

~244~

Have you ever experienced the sweet gaze of Jesus?

Suddenly, you feel a certain indescribable tenderness. It's a difficult experience to explain. It had happened to me on a few occasions, but I didn't know what it was. I was driving the car and suddenly a happiness flooded my soul. It was very brief, and I never understood what it was. As the years passed, it happened again. But this time I knew.

"It was You," I said to Jesus, smiling with joy.

I stayed silently looking at Him, in that Holy Host. He looked at me, and I looked at Him. Words were unnecessary. The whole world revolved around us.

Recently, it happened again.

"You call me, Jesus," I said.

And I went to a little chapel to accompany Him for a while in prayer. I discovered Him alone in that Tabernacle.

Now I make an effort to visit Him frequently. He deserves all our love and more. Jesus continues to touch souls and transform the hearts of many people around us. How good You are, Lord!

~245~

Recently, I attended a Eucharistic celebration where some young people were concluding their spiritual retreat. One of the young participants stood at the podium and shared her experience.

"I came, like many, out of obligation. I didn't feel anything special. But on the last day, when the priest processed with the Blessed Sacrament among us, suddenly, in a fraction of a second, when Jesus was beside me, I experienced such intense, profound peace... Like I had never experienced before. It was as if Jesus was speaking to me. It was wonderful."

Truly, Jesus, you are wonderful.

Thank you for your infinite love and for your consolations. Thank you for loving us with such love.

~246~

How is it possible that God loves us so much?
How is such great love possible?

I come from the Tabernacle in a nearby chapel near my house. I love visiting Jesus. I recommend to everyone I can: "Go, visit Jesus, tell Him everything. He will fill you with favors, abundant graces, and give you the strength you need to move forward. And when you leave, as a favor, tell Him:

"Good Jesus, Claudio sends his greetings."

I have spent the last few days immersed in His loving gaze. I am a man lost in the desert who found an oasis of peace in that chapel and no longer wishes to leave it. All because of a simple visit to Jesus in the Blessed Sacrament. A brief moment when I told Him I loved Him. That was enough to leave me restless, with a sweetness in my soul...

I love the words of Saint Alphonsus, they are so true, I have proven them so many times:

"Oh, if only men would always turn to the Most Blessed Sacrament to seek the remedy for their troubles, surely, they would not be as unhappy as they are!"

~248~

Whenever you can, visit Jesus in the Blessed Sacrament. He waits for you in the Tabernacle. I often visit Him and find Him alone.

As Blessed María Romero used to say: "Jesus desires to find our heart expanded with love and trust, adorned with humility, chastity, and purity."

Will you offer Him a pure and humble heart?

Will you trust in Jesus?

Will you visit Him in the Tabernacle?

~249~

Sometimes, when I have a very serious problem and the world seems to be collapsing around me, I repeat to myself: "Trust, Claudio. Trust in God. You must have faith." Then, serenity arrives. Strength. Peace. And we can face the situation by finding the best solution. The truth is, I don't like going through these trials, but they are part of life. It's God's pedagogy. His way of strengthening our faith, leading us to a level of holiness that we could never reach on our own.

I've realized that God makes the souls He loves the most go through great adversities. It's His pedagogy. Just read the life of any saint to understand. Padre Pio was made to endure a difficult life for 10 years, the Servant of God María Romero faced great trials, John Paul II experienced suffering and illness. As Saint Teresa said, "Still waters become stagnant and stale. Water must flow to remain clear."

When you pass through adversity, you can say to yourself as Sister María Romero did: "God wills it. So do I." Why? Perhaps we will only know in heaven. Clay is not in a position to judge the potter. It must be surrendered into His skillful hands, which will shape it beautifully. When pain is not understood, the best course is to offer it up.

~250~

"Remain in my love." John 15:9

Some years ago, I discovered a devout practice that I have not ceased to follow to this day. It is Spiritual Communion. "Spiritual communion," wrote Saint Alphonsus, "is a burning desire to receive Jesus in the Blessed Sacrament and lovingly embrace Him at least spiritually, as if we had actually received Him." Many saints and priests have spoken to us about this devotion, encouraging us to practice it. Saint Josemaría Escrivá also wrote about this admirable mystery that grants us the graces of the Eucharistic communion. "What a source of grace is Spiritual Communion! Practice it frequently and you will have more of God's presence and closer union with Him in your actions." Through a sincere desire to receive Him, Jesus grants you grace. He gives everything for the souls He loves so much. It is enough that you desire Him. His Mercy knows no bounds. While it does not give us the fullness of the sacrament, it helps us to grow in sanctifying grace, unites us with Jesus, and enlivens in us a thirst for God.

When for some reason I have been unable to receive Eucharistic communion, Spiritual Communion remains for me. I highly recommend it, especially to those who cannot receive sacramental communion.

Sometimes, while driving my car, I pause and repeat the formula I learned for making a Spiritual Communion. Also, during Mass, at the moment when the priest elevates the consecrated Host. What a moment! Jesus knows how to ignite our hearts and plants in our souls the fervent desire to receive Him... sweet guest of the soul! It is a prayer, simple in itself, yet how effective! In his beautiful book "Visits to the Blessed Sacrament," Saint Alphonsus Maria de Liguori reminds us of the importance of Spiritual Communions, particularly when we visit Jesus in the Blessed Sacrament. It is a beautiful devotion that bears many spiritual fruits. Have you ever tried it? I strive to do it daily. I have discovered an endless source of graces that help me to be closer to Jesus. You can make Spiritual Communions throughout the day as often as you wish. Are you interested?

SPIRITUAL COMMUNION

My Jesus, I believe that You are present
in the Most Holy Sacrament.
I love You above all things,
and I desire to receive You into my soul.
Since I cannot at this moment receive You
sacramentally, come at least spiritually
into my heart. I embrace You as if You were
already there and unite myself wholly to You.
Never permit me to be separated from You.
Amen.

~251~

This is a very simple prayer that pleases Jesus and that we can pray during our visits to the Blessed Sacrament. You don't need many words when you're with Jesus. He knows everything, He knows your heart. Your love is enough for Him, your sincere desire to change, to be better, to seek Him. I know Jesus will be very happy when He sees you enter the chapel and kneel before Him. Tell Him that you love Him. If you could hear Him, He would surely say to you: 'I have been waiting for you for so long.'

My Lord Jesus Christ,
I adore you in all the tabernacles of the world.
I offer you my life in reparation for the sins
against the Blessed Sacrament,
the unworthy communions, disrespect,
lack of reverence in your churches,
and countless other sins against
your most Holy Body and Blood.
Please, my Lord, increase my faith
in your Eucharistic presence
so that my devotion may be fanned
into a flame of love of you
and that I may go into the world
to proclaim your kingdom.
I ask this of your mercy
in your Holy Name. Amen. Mary,
Mother of the Eucharist, pray for us!

~252~

When I was young, I studied in a Catholic school. Sweet nuns taught us our lessons. It was a time of purity of heart, when everything was simpler, and the thought of offending God never crossed our minds. Despite the years that have passed, I can still remember Sister Maria Avila from the Order of St. Francis of Assisi. It was a different summer morning when she entered the classroom to explain to us:

'Jesus remains for us in the tabernacles of the Churches. His love is so great that He has chosen to stay in the holy host. How can we recognize Him? Every time you enter a Church, look for a small lamp lit beside the Tabernacle. It's called the lamp of the Blessed Sacrament. It will indicate to you the presence of the Blessed Sacrament. If for any reason the Lord is not in the Tabernacle, you will find it extinguished.'

Since then, it's the first thing I do when I enter a Church. 'Where are you?' I ask Him, while searching for the lit lamp. When I finally see it, relieved, I smile.'Here you are,' I say to Him. And I greet Him. And it seems He responds: 'For you and for all the people I love so much, I remain in the Tabernacles, even in the most forgotten ones where no one visits me.'"

~253~

I wonder what would happen if we could see with the eyes of the soul. The Tabernacle would surely shine with a celestial glow, emanating from it rays of multicolored light, countless and endless.

Hundreds of thousands of angels would be constantly in Your presence, guarding and praising Your majesty with songs of: 'Glory, glory, glory to the Lamb of God, who takes away the sins of the world.' But our mortal eyes do not allow us to see beyond.

~254~

One morning I reflected on the difficulties we face each day, on how hard life can be, on the work ahead of us, on misunderstandings... on my lack of faith, and I found myself saying this prayer to God, which came straight from my heart and now I share with you:

IT'S SO HARD, LORD

It's hard for me to do what You ask of me.
It's hard for me to love those who hurt me.
It's hard for me to forgive.
It's hard for me to get up every time I fall.
It's hard for me to trust...
It's hard for me to surrender daily,
and to experience Your loving presence.
It's so hard, Lord...
Dwell in me, as You do
in my brothers and sisters.
Fill us with Your presence.
Surround us in Your grace.
Show me Your ways.
Tell me what You want,
and I will do it,
even if I don't like it,
even if I don't understand it,
even if I don't want to.
I will do it just because You ask me to.

~255~

There are truly surprising stories about people who, at some point in their lives, have been touched by the unfathomable love of God. I have known many such cases and can attest to this: "Truly, no one remains indifferent in the presence of the living Jesus in the Blessed Sacrament."

At the age of 26, on a Friday in May 1847, Hermann Cohen, a musician and practicing Jew, directed the choir at the Church of Sainte-Valérie in Paris, filling in for a friend who had asked him for a favor. Something exceptional happened to him that day which would change his life. "I accepted, inspired solely by love for musical art," Hermann wrote, "and out of the satisfaction of doing a favor. When the moment of the Blessing of the Most Holy Sacrament arrived, I experienced an indescribable disturbance. I found myself compelled to bend towards the ground, against my own will. I returned the following Friday and was similarly impressed, and suddenly the idea of becoming Catholic occurred to me." On August 8th of the same year, Hermann was in Ems to give a concert and attended Sunday Mass at the small Catholic church in the city. At the elevation of the Sacred Host, he could not hold back a torrent of tears. "There, little by little, the chants, the prayers, the invisible yet felt presence of a superhuman power began to stir me, to disturb me, to make me tremble. In a word, divine grace delighted in pouring itself upon me with all its force. At the moment of the elevation, through my eyelids, I suddenly felt a flood of tears spring forth that continued to flow down my cheeks..." Spontaneously, as if by intuition, I began to make a general confession to God of all the enormous faults committed since my childhood: I saw them there, spread out before me, by the thousands, hideous, repulsive... And yet I also felt, through an unknown calm that poured its balm into my soul, that merciful God would forgive me, that He would take pity on my sincere contrition, on my bitter pain...

Yes, I felt forgiven, and that He accepted my firm will to love Him above all things and to henceforth unite myself with Him. Upon leaving that church in Ems, I was already a Christian at heart..."

This Jewish convert to Catholicism founded the Night Adoration, "an association for the Exposition and Night Adoration of the Most Holy Sacrament, for the reparation of the outrages it suffers, and to attract upon France and the world the blessings of God and to avert from it the evils that threaten." It quickly spread throughout all Catholic countries up to our days. If we understood the value and graces obtained through the Adoration of the Most Holy Sacrament, we would never cease to adore and accompany Jesus.

(Source: www.clairval.com)

~256~

I have endeavored to dedicate more time to prayer. Having a brief prayer on my lips, saying it like breathing, with the naturalness of the breath that gives us life. And then visiting Jesus and continuing with a:

"Jesus, I love you," and then a "How good you are, Lord," or "Your grace is worth more than life."

Sometimes, when I visit him, Jesus touches our hearts. It is very warm and tender. I already know him. You don't understand at the moment what is happening to you. It is an unheard-of happiness. Like a longing that you have achieved.

I always find the answers to my concerns in the Bible and the Tabernacle, where Jesus lives, alive.

~257~

Has it happened to you?

You change. You feel different. Everything seems wonderful to you. You start enjoying sunrises again. You are happy, with a happiness and inner joy that you had forgotten when facing so many difficulties in life.

This happens when you start attending daily Mass and visiting Jesus in the Tabernacle. At first, you live by grace, under God's paternal care. He indulges you and Providence abounds. Everything is marvelous.

Every day is a miracle, a gesture of God's love towards humanity. Over time, you will live by faith, knowing that you are not alone, that God dwells within you, cares for you, and loves you.

~258~

CHILDHOOD PRAYERS

There are moments in our lives when we return to our childhood, when we were happy, and everything seemed simple. Today it happened to me. Since I woke up, I have rediscovered little Claudio, the child I once was, when the world was a pure and simple place, when what I longed for the most was to be with Jesus. When I studied with the Franciscan nuns at Paulino of Saint Joseph school in the city of Colon. For some reason, the good God has granted me this grace. To see myself as a child, innocent, fully trusting in His Fatherly love.

I knew something special awaited me in the old bookshelf, and there I went to find who knows what. It didn't take long to find a small, somewhat worn book titled "My Little Heart Prays". It was published in 1953, and since Sister Ávila gave it to me, I have never been apart from it.

I told my wife, "Look what I found," "the booklet from my first communion." I opened it to find the memories. Little Claudio, coming out of the chapel, shorts and a great emotion in his heart and soul. I brought my Lord for the first time, like a living tabernacle. That sunny morning, I received my first communion. I was happy, with my little book in hand. The world and heaven belonged to me. I needed nothing more. On page 31, there is a beautiful postcard of a child's room. A small, neatly made bed, a cross on the wall, a picture of the Sacred Heart of Jesus. And the text says, "A Catholic Child's Room." Does your room resemble a Catholic child's room? Does your room have a crucifix on the wall? Do you have holy water in your room? Do you have any holy images on the wall? Do you have a small altar for prayer? Do you keep your room tidy and clean?

I took my book to Mass that day and on the way, I prayed:

"Good Saint Joseph…
Teach me not to be afraid of work.
Teach me to be honest.
Teach me to be kind to the poor.
Teach me to love Jesus and Mary.
Good Saint Joseph, bless my home."

The Mass was particularly beautiful. Before communion, I looked for my booklet and prayed:

"Right now, on the altar
the bread and wine were changed
into the body and blood of Christ.
My Jesus, I believe this with all my heart.
I believe in God, the Father Almighty;
I believe that you are the Son of God;

I believe in the Holy Spirit.
I believe in these truths because
You have told us so. And your words are true."

After such an anticipated and desired communion, I knelt to adore and tell Him that I loved Him.

"A thousand and a thousand times
welcome my dear Jesus.
You are now in my poor heart.
You have filled it with joys,
and I am very happy.
Stay in my heart.
Make my heart yours forever and ever."

"I noticed," my wife said when we left Mass. "Something special has happened today."

"Yes," I replied excitedly.

Once again, Jesus and I were the great friends, childhood friends, ready to go into the world, carrying His Love.

~259~

There are moments
that belong only to God.

Then, words are unnecessary.

It's enough to love
with all your heart
and all your soul
the Good Lord.

~260~

The woman who trusts in God is recognized because she radiates peace and serenity. Her words always deeply touch the soul because they carry truth. Few earthly things disturb her. She experiences the infinite love of God in her daily life. It's a very intimate and fraternal relationship, and she converses naturally:

"Look, Jesus, this happened to me at work."
"Help me, Jesus, to solve this problem."
"Jesus, did you like that?"

She experiences this sweet certainty: "Jesus loves me." That's why she dares to be different and is a sign of contradiction in this materialistic world.

Are you encouraged to follow Jesus?

~261~

The guard angrily pounded on the bars of the cell. He used the metal plate from the butt of his rifle to make more noise. A faint light illuminated the place. It was gloomy like all prisons and dungeons of dictators, designed to instill fear.

"Stand up and come closer," ordered the jailer authoritatively. The prisoner, Dr. Carlos Ivan Zuñiga, slowly got up from the bunk, took a few steps, and leaned on the rusted bars of the door.

"Do you remember me, doctor?" asked the guard, pointing the rifle at him. There was much hatred in his words. The prisoner was my wife Vida's uncle. He was taken to a special prison where politicians with libertarian ideas were locked up during the nascent military dictatorship that lasted 21 years in my country.

This story is true. It was told to me by Dr. Zuñiga himself, years later, one night at his farm.

"I'm afraid I don't remember," he replied.

"Years ago, when you were a young lawyer, you incriminated me in a criminal case. I was declared guilty and served five years. I got out of prison and joined the national army. They assigned me as a guard in this place. When I found out you were imprisoned here, I decided to take revenge. I will harm you, doctor, with this rifle, be sure of that. But first, I want you to suffer. That's why you won't know when I will come to take my revenge. It will be at any moment, and no one will notice you're dead until the next day."

Weeks passed in uncertainty and confinement in that dark cell. Eventually, he was allowed weekly visits from his family.

Vida, my wife, who was just a child at the time, sent him a letter to encourage him. When his wife and their five young children arrived at the prison, they encountered a sweet elderly woman they knew well at the entrance.

She was the gatekeeper who greeted them lovingly every morning at school. The children, thrilled to see her, surrounded her with joyous hugs.

"Hello, hello... How wonderful!"

That night, the guard arrived at Dr. Zuñiga's cell again. This time, he didn't carry his threatening rifle but a plate of freshly prepared hot food.

"From now on, I will be your protector, doctor, and no one will dare to mess with you."

"And what's the reason for this admirable change?"

"This morning, my mother came to visit me. She encountered your children at the entrance. They expressed so much joy and love to her, happily embracing her. Their beautiful gesture towards my mother, the happiness they gave her, the love they felt for her, touched my heart and erased my resentment and hatred towards you. That's why I decided to look after you and ensure you safely leave this hellish place. Count on me for whatever you need from now on."

The night Carlos Ivan told us his story, we were all stunned. We kept a deep and respectful silence, unsure of what to say.

It was true what Saint Therese of Lisieux asserted:

"Love has no limits, no boundaries, no barriers. Love is for everyone and is capable of transforming lives."

In this case, the love of his children for the guard's mother saved Dr. Zuñiga's life.

I remember thinking, "Love is a gift, an extraordinary grace, capable of transforming and melting the hardest hearts."

~262~

Last night I thought about how extraordinary life is. I spent a long time in prayer. It was a wonderful conversation with God, in the midst of the night and the silence. As time passed, I realized that I am like a cracked jar, waiting for the potter to mend it. I became aware of my lack of faith.

To truly be happy, I must learn to trust in God's promises: "Therefore do not worry, saying, 'What shall we eat?' or 'What shall we drink?' or 'What shall we wear?' For after all these things the Gentiles seek. For your heavenly Father knows that you need all these things. But seek first the kingdom of God and His righteousness, and all these things shall be added to you" (Matthew 6:31, 33).

I want to learn about love. To leave my home every morning, loving my fellow human beings. To have charity. To bring God to my brothers, those who live alone, those who suffer, those who have not felt the embrace of a friend. The hours passed and everything was silent until dawn. Suddenly, I understood: It was true what Saint Teresa said: "God alone is enough." You need nothing more.

A great hope invaded me. A supernatural peace. Immense joy. Could it be the presence of God? It was as if a flame ignited my heart. A need to love emerged suddenly, and I realized: "The way is love. The meaning of life is love." That flame, which we all carry, must be nurtured, used to set this weary world on fire with the fire and love of God. At dawn, I left behind uncertainty and fear and began to walk anew. This time more assured, more confident, because I know we are not alone. Man is not alone. God accompanies him.

~263~

I've spent a few days away from the city and the noise. I decided it would be a encounter with God. Somehow I would meet Him. And I found no better way than prayer.

In the mornings, I went for walks with my wife Vida and spoke to God within me, as naturally as a child to their father. Over time, I fell silent. Instead of speaking, I let Him dwell within me. It was like opening the doors of your home to a long-awaited guest. That's how I opened my soul and asked Him to dwell in me.

On the final stretch of the journey, I felt embraced, loved from eternity. His presence was so strong, His love so great, that it overwhelmed my smallness. I walked the path with overflowing happiness.

I felt serene, secure, peaceful. Trusting in the One who cared for me and was in me, with me, by my side, all around me. A God Almighty, omnipresent, who encompasses everything and treats us with eternal, unconditional love. I often say, "How good that God is good." You don't know how much it moves me to know He is my Father, your Father, our Father.

~264~

"God speaks to us in the silence of the heart. If you are before God in prayer and silence, He will speak to you; then, you will know that you are nothing. And only when we understand our nothingness, our emptiness, can God fill us with Himself. Prayerful souls are souls of great silence."

Mother Teresa of Calcutta

~265~

This morning, as I returned from my usual walk, I thought with excitement, "We must nourish ourselves with You, Lord. You give us the strength to live, to continue our struggles, to not become discouraged. Only You are the answer to our concerns." This experience is not new. Meeting God is a vital necessity. Moses went up a mountain to speak alone with God. Jesus used to spend nights in prayer in the Garden of Gethsemane. Laypeople, monks, and nuns discovered this encounter with the Father centuries ago. Many would go to a cave in solitude to reflect and think about God, to live immersed in His loving presence. That's why retreats are so beneficial. They allow you to be alone with God away from distractions. They help you deepen your intimacy with God and receive His grace, recognizing it. We cannot withdraw to a mountain and have those intense experiences because the world and times have changed. Everything is more hectic now. There is little time to be alone with God. We have to live in the world "without being of the world." We must carry within us that "flame" of God's love, guard it, not let it extinguish. And ignite other fires, other hearts around us. Show everyone that it is possible, that we can live loving God and our neighbors. That we can forgive and forget offenses, that we are capable of turning the other cheek in the face of insults. That we are called to live as children of the Most High God.

~266~

"Be perfect, therefore, as your heavenly Father is perfect." Matthew 5:48

God does not ask the impossible of us. He asks us for holiness, for perfection, because it is possible. And He gives us the graces and virtues to achieve it.

Don't settle for being good. Take one more small step, a little more love, and you will achieve what God desires so much from you. We are called to Love. That is our goal. To love.

I have often thought that it is something so difficult, not impossible, but challenging. Perhaps with our own strength we may never succeed, but with God by our side, everything will be easier, purer.

~267~

"Enter through the narrow gate. For wide is the gate and broad is the road that leads to destruction, and many enter through it." (Matthew 7)

God's paths are narrow and wonderful. They are challenging but at the same time fill you with peace and joy.

~268~

It used to happen to me that suddenly I would be flooded with a happiness, an indescribable joy, something that surpassed my strength and I didn't know what it was. I just wanted to stay like that, without moving, enjoying this wonderful experience. Over time, I could recognize what was happening to me. More than an experience, it was a presence. His presence. God was there, with me. He passed by and transformed everything around Him. I love to imagine God walking among us, as He did in the Garden of Eden. He passes by and transforms everything in His path. My wife has an aunt who grows coffee and oranges. One summer, we visited her with our children. She took us to harvest oranges for breakfast. As she walked, she would say aloud, "Jesus passed through here." She told us that since she started praying in this way, the orange groves had doubled their production and provided a juice as sweet and pleasant as honey. This incomparable presence of God has impacted hundreds of people over centuries and transforms them. Suddenly, they change and become better people to everyone's surprise. Those who have experienced God no longer desire anything but to love Him. It's as if we have a seed of goodness stored within us and God passes by our side commanding, "It's time to sprout." And this small seed, which we didn't even notice, suddenly sprouts in our souls and goes from being a forgotten seed to a tender plant, and finally, a healthy, robust, immovable tree.

~269~

In October 1999, I was in the radio station booth talking about Jesus, about how wonderful He is, about how gently He leads you to lose your fears, to make up your mind, and take the leap towards conversion, and then towards a life leading to holiness.

I presented Jesus, the good and tender Friend, a true friend who will never harm you, who only wants the best for you. Occasionally, I would play a song and then continue talking about Jesus.

Suddenly, I received a phone call. It seemed to be from a young woman who was moved. Her voice was sweet yet sad: "Is it true," she asked tearfully, "what you say about Jesus?" "Oh yes," I responded excitedly, "it's all true. And I know it not because someone told me, but because I am living it. From experience, I know you can trust Jesus."

There was a pause, and both of us fell silent, as if our hearts were in the Heart of Jesus.

Finally, I said to her: "Take courage, have faith. Jesus will never abandon you."

That night, I left the radio station feeling happy, as if the world had been transformed. And I thought about the soul of that young woman, filled with hope in Jesus.

~270~

A Biblical advice

"¿Is anyone among you suffering?
He should pray.

James 5

~271~

Have you noticed the happiness on a child's face? How delightful it is to live with a pure soul!

Their hearts and minds are often not in this world. They inhabit different planets than ours, more joyful, where understanding and hope abound. That's why they play carefree, oblivious to their surroundings. The saints have discovered this reality. They know well, "we are not of this world." They live despising what the earth offers them: fame, money, possessions... They aspire to something much better, eternal, infinite, all-powerful: "God." That's why, amidst their absolute poverty, they are happy. Haven't you read about the adventures of St. Francis of Assisi? Poor, without material possessions, yet happier than anyone. He trusted completely in Divine Providence. He gave himself entirely to God. And God did not disappoint him. To be saved, humans must turn their gaze to God. Repentant, change their lives, be born again. This is what we are called to: to be born again, to be holy, pure, and good. We do not belong to this world; we are only passing through, on our way to Heaven. We must not allow the accidents of the journey to cause us to perish along the way, losing our eternal life through sin. What happens when you break your covenant with God? Well, you start to sin, and one sin leads to another worse one. If we are dirty, we think that by getting a little dirtier, no one will notice. However, any sin, no matter how small it seems, is something awful and terrible in the eyes of the Creator who is Holy, Just, and Good. By sinning, we lose part of our capacity to receive God's grace. We limit our spiritual life. We weaken ourselves. We walk crippled, deformed, sick, and dirty. There's something important you should know: God hates sin, but loves the sinner. God does not approve of your sins, but He loves you and indulges you as if you were a child. You are His favorite. You are called to a mission, a woman of faith, to discover His calling and then obey it. Almost all missions are alike, but they are different. They have something in common: "to serve and to love." When you cleanse your soul with a good confession before a priest (he is the only one on earth who can forgive your sins), you will begin to understand. And a new world will open before your eyes. You will experience the grace that only God can give, enriching our lives and strengthening our souls. God is good and He loves you. My experience is similar to that of the psalmist (Psalm 25) when he wrote: "No one who hopes in you will ever be put to shame." I have never been disappointed by God, although I have disappointed Him. Trusting in God, seeking Him, is a wonderful thing that you must live, to have the experience.

Try it out. Trust in Him. God will never disappoint you.

~272~

In your home,
do you pray the Holy Rosary?

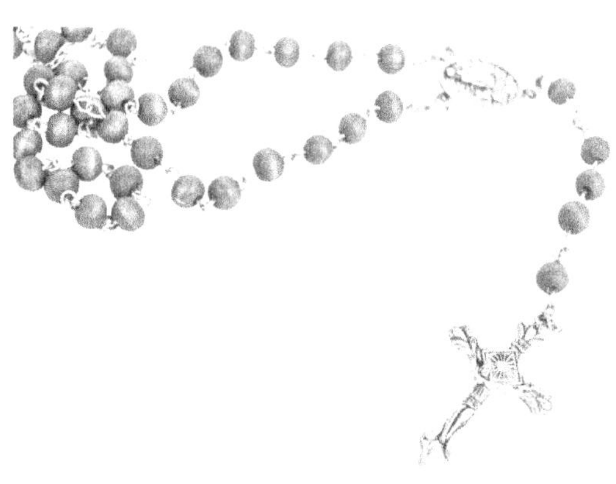

~273~

Once I spent the day restless. I was seeking answers, but not always in the right place. In the afternoon, I took my Bible to a nearby chapel. I opened it at random and found these words that restored my peace:

Thus says the Lord:

"Stand at the crossroads and look; ask for the ancient paths, ask where the good way is, and walk in it, and you will find rest for your souls." (Jeremiah 6:16)

~274~

Once I heard someone say that God doesn't send telegrams or messages to direct us towards our vocation. If only we knew Him a little better! He is very creative and has marvelous ways of communicating with us. A family member recently emailed me about the extraordinary experience they had with God:

"Yesterday, while I was at the office, my wife called me to give me information about a job posting. I noted down the phone number and the contact's name and prepared to make the call. I dialed the number (or so I thought), and a voice of a lady, not very old but rather mature, answered with the following dialogue:

— Good afternoon. Is Mr. Perez available?
— No, he is not. What is the matter regarding?
— It's about the job posting.
— What kind of job is it???
— It's for Visual Fox Pro programming.
— Look, that's not here, but I have a message from the lord for you...

I found the response so contradictory, but honestly, I was thinking about the gentleman with a lowercase 'l'. She continued, with a very tender voice, saying the following:

— He says He still loves you unconditionally and holds you close to His Immaculate Heart.

At that moment, I understood that the gentleman she was talking about was spelled with an uppercase 'L'. She ended with a 'God bless you', to which I responded, 'Thank you very much!'

My whole being trembled from head to toe, and tears welled up in my eyes. Those words had touched the deepest fibers of my being, those that only God can touch, and I found myself crying in that office in the midst of my workday. Psalm 8 came to mind, and I remembered how my mother always told me that when I read the Bible, I should place myself in the passage; for all the promises contained therein are for me, so I did, and from my whole soul came the following prayer:

'O Lord, our Lord, How majestic is your name in all the earth! You have set your glory above the heavens... When I consider your heavens, the work of your fingers, the moon and the stars, which you have set in place, what is mankind that you are mindful of them, human beings that you care for them? You have made them a little lower than the angels and crowned them with glory and honor. O Lord, our Lord, How majestic is your name in all the earth!'

Then I dialed again, and this time a man's voice answered... It was Mr. Perez, arranging an interview for next Monday. I learned something important: it doesn't matter if I get the job; it was enough to know that God heard my prayer!"

I often meet a friend who marvels at the discoveries he has made within our Holy Mother Church: Peace. Interior life. The sacraments.

"They are the great treasures of the Church," I tell him. "It's like an open chest, full of treasures available to us. But many don't know it's there.

~275~

When I was a child, we used to attend early Sunday Mass. Even though my dad was Hebrew, he would come with us. I loved it because afterwards he would treat us to ice cream and a delicious, still-warm apple pie they served at the Christian Youth Club in Colón. Perhaps because of this beautiful memory, I often take my kids for ice cream after Mass. You should see how much we enjoy it. Sometimes, if I forget, they remind me:

"Dad..., ice cream."

And off we go right away.

They grow up so fast. It feels like just yesterday I was carrying my little son proudly on my shoulders for a walk. Son and father. But we hadn't even reached the corner when he would rest his little head and fall asleep.

Now he's a big boy, and we enjoy the activities we can do together. My friends, who already have grown-up kids, remind me daily:

"Enjoy them, because life passes by so quickly."

It's true, life passes by so quickly. And suddenly we realize we've aged. It's been like a sigh. But a long and pleasant sigh, in which we've been able to recognize God's tenderness. How good He is.

Yes, there comes a moment when you understand the psalmist who emotionally sings: "When anxiety was great within me, your consolation brought me joy." (Psalm 94)

I recognize His presence in the smiles of my children when they wake up in the morning and come to greet us with such excitement; when the youngest one sneaks into our bed at night and you realize it's because he wants to hug you.

They are no longer babies. But the world still intrigues them. There's so much to discover. I join them in this quest and rediscover the world.

I used to drive the youngest one to school. He's quite talkative, and during the journey, he would spot dogs, cats, a new tree, a kid who hadn't yet caught the school bus...

But one day he was silent, lost in thought. I watched him through the rearview mirror and felt concerned. Something was bothering him. Suddenly he broke the silence and asked anxiously:

"Dad, when I grow up, will I also be bald?"

"No, my king, Dad is not bald," I replied. "It's just that Mom cuts my hair very short."

"Ohhh..." he sighed in relief. "That's good!"

~276~

Are you going through a tough time? God's message has arrived for you.

"Do not fear, for I am with you..."

(Isaiah 41:10)

~277~

Life is curious; you look at your newborn son and before you know it, you're sitting beside him in the car, all grown up, teaching him to drive. You know he'll soon leave home to build his own life. You wonder when it all happened. That's how it happened to me. How good God is!

In the photo, I am with my fourth son, Luis Felipe. He's already 20 years old. Time passes very quickly, so it's important to enjoy them every day.

~278~

Strive for the eternal. Sometimes I sit and reflect, and I think, "What will Paradise be like? Spending eternity in heaven, beside the one who loves us above all things." Can you imagine it?

In those sad days, your comfort
will be the Eucharist.

~279~

A woman of faith seeks to please God in everything.

~280~

The ideal is to reach heaven and find souls that you helped with your prayer, with a timely word, with a kind gesture, with your own example.

~281~

There is a deep silence in the house. Everyone is lying in their bed, ready to sleep. Suddenly, a discovery, and from the smallest child's room comes an excited cry: "28 days until my birthday! How happy!"

We, with that childish purity, should also shout to the four winds: "How happy I am! God loves me!"

~282~

I often think about our weakness. We are like clay jars that hold a great treasure. We are temples of the Holy Spirit when we are in God's grace. And yet, we fall and fall again. I believe it's because we pray so little.

We talk with friends, neighbors, and relatives, but we talk very little with God. We lack prayer. If I were a doctor, I would prescribe "a little prayer" to every patient who visited me. In prayer, I have found strength for difficult times. And I have managed to move forward with God's grace. Purely by grace. And by His goodness.

Recently, I approached a painting I have of Jesus. I love looking at Him and chatting with Him. It might sound silly, but He is my best friend. How could I not talk to Him? I looked into His eyes, and this prayer came from my soul...

"LET ME LOSE EVERYTHING, BUT NOT YOUR FRIENDSHIP

Lord, you know that I am made of clay and at some point I will fall. Surely sin will lead me away from you. That's why I ask you: "Let me lose everything but not your friendship." You are my best friend. How could I lose you? I know I don't always do what I should. Even so, I try to follow you. Believe me, Lord, I try. But you see, I am so weak, So fragile. And I fear losing you.

Today I have come to you, Repentant, desolate, to look into your eyes, and tell you that I love you.

But it has been you who looked into my eyes. With so much tenderness. With so much love. That from my soul came out this cry:

"Lord, let me lose everything, but not your friendship."

~283~

A holy priest, Father Alberto Hurtado, wrote:

— Do not hesitate! Fight bravely to follow Christ's call.

Here then we can pose the crucial question: What does Christ want from me? Have you asked Jesus yet? I remember well one afternoon when I dared to do so. It was just Him and me. Kneeling before the Blessed Sacrament, deeply moved, I asked Him:

— Lord, what do you want from me?

It seemed to me that I heard a gentle inner voice affectionately responding:

— That you do good.

This short life deserves to be lived intensely, for God, and by God. Under His loving and tender gaze.

In a part of the city, there is a convent school where nuns dedicate themselves to caring for orphaned girls and those from underprivileged backgrounds. At the entrance, there is a small image of Saint Euphrasia, their founder. She holds an open book in her hand, and on it, these words can be read:

~285~

"If we confess our sins, he who is faithful and just will forgive us our sins and cleanse us from all unrighteousness." 1 John 1:9

"Did you know that you can be saved if you are in danger of death and there is no priest nearby to hear your confession?"

The Pope has explained it clearly:

"Do what the Catechism tells you. It is very clear what it says there: if you cannot find a priest to hear your confession, speak with God, who is your Father, and tell Him the truth. List your sins, ask the Lord for forgiveness with all your heart, and make an act of contrition. Promise Him: 'I will confess later but forgive me now.' And immediately the grace of God will be back within you."

What does the Catechism of the Church say?

1452 When it arises from a love by which God is loved above all else, contrition is called "perfect" (contrition of charity). Such contrition forgives venial sins; it also obtains forgiveness of mortal sins if it includes the firm resolution to have recourse to sacramental confession as soon as possible.

~286~

A LITTLE ADVICE?

With so much traffic congestion, work difficulties, family arguments, shopping trips to malls, you need a bit of peace.

Take a moment to go to a CHAPEL where they have Jesus in the TABERNACLE. You need silence, peace, serenity, prayer. Be SILENT and accompany Jesus. It will RENEW your life.

Tell me later how it went.

~287~

"Then I saw a river
that every soul must cross
to reach the Kingdom of Heaven.
And the name of that river was:

'Suffering.'

Then I saw a boat
that carried souls across the river.
And the name of that boat was:

'LOVE.'

Saint John of the Cross

~288~

THE ADVICE OF A SAINT:

"When you feel the pride boiling within you – the arrogance! – that makes you consider yourself a superman, it is time to exclaim: no! And thus, you will savor the joy of being a good child of God, who walks on earth with mistakes, but doing good."

Saint Josemaría Escrivá

~289~

FROM JESUS TO YOU

I love you. I want you to know.
You are special to me.

Don't know where to take refuge?
Immerse yourself in my Love.

Your indifference pains me.

Sin separates you from me.

When I was on the cross,
I was thinking of you.

You are not alone.
I am always with you.

~290~

To something great and wonderful you were born: ETERNITY.

~291~

"When we were small, we used to cling to our mother when passing through dark paths or where there were dogs. Now, when feeling the temptations of the flesh, we must cling closely to Our Mother of Heaven, through her close presence and through ejaculatory prayers. She will defend us and lead us into the light."

St. Josemaria Escriva

~292~

From Jesus to you:

Imagine what I feel for you,
waiting for you in the Tabernacle,
to fill you with graces.

I want you to forgive everyone.
Always, at all times.
And love them all.
Always, at all times,]as I have loved them.

To anyone who tells you,
"You are worth nothing,"
you will reply:
"I am worth everything.
I am a child of God."

What is most important to my Father?
You.

You have always been and will always be
the most Important to God.

~293~

From Jesus to you:

A soul in love is not afraid.
It accepts everything gladly.
And always surrenders into God's hands.

Never forget that I also died for your sins.

How can you live in peace, i
f God does not dwell in your heart?

Trust in God and do good.
Trust and leave your worries to my Father.
Trust and my Father will provide.

Do you see?
Everything is easier
after having prayed.

~294~

From Jesus to you:

I demand acts of mercy from you, which must be performed out of love for Me. You must show mercy to your neighbor always and everywhere. Do not be afraid of this or try to excuse yourself or exempt yourself from it. I am giving you three ways to exercise mercy toward your neighbor:

- The first is by deed,
- The second by word,
- And the third by prayer.

In these three degrees is contained the fullness of mercy and it is a proof of your love for Me.

(Diary of Saint Faustina No. 742)

~295~

It's time to abandon theory and live our faith. It's time to lead a sacramental life and commit to being saints. It's time to live for God, in His presence, and be an inspiring force for others. It's time to trust in God and believe in His promises.

It's time to approach the poor with love and selflessness. It's time to see Christ in the poor. It's time to forgive and ask for forgiveness. It's time to forget offenses and move forward. It's time to show the world that God is our Father, a kind and tender father. It's time to pray and converse with God. It's time to turn our gaze to the Father. It's time to know His Word and experience His Tenderness and Love. It's time to work for the Kingdom. It's time now to love our neighbor, for who they are: our brother.

It is God's time and ours, because we are His children and were created for eternity.

~296~

How difficult it is to achieve serenity. Moments of tribulation lurk around every corner. Saint Francis of Assisi said that perfect joy is to accept willingly everything that happens to us, offering it for the glory of God, who always knows how to bring good out of bad. But it is so hard for me. Therefore, I have resolved to bless when I feel like cursing, to forgive when reason urges me to hate. I have resolved to leave everything in God's hands. To learn to trust. It is necessary to endure bitter moments if you want to be a disciple of Jesus.

What more can we expect? We are disciples of the crucified. We hope to resemble Him. "Man of sorrows." The disciple always longs to resemble his Master. With these thoughts, I decided to visit Jesus in the Blessed Sacrament. He always has the answers. He knows what to do. He is my friend. And I love Him very much. I entered the church in pain, striving to forgive. Then I found pamphlets about the Claretian martyrs of Barbastro, sacrificed during the Spanish Civil War. A priest killed in August 1936 was speaking to me. A few brief words of his were enough for me to accompany him in his pain as he awaited his execution. He taught me to forgive. I understood that what I go through is nothing compared to what they had to endure. Such faith, such courage...

"We spend the day in religious silence and preparing to die tomorrow.

Only the holy murmur of prayers is felt in this room, witness of our harsh anxieties.

If we speak, it is to encourage ourselves to die as martyrs.

If we pray, it is to forgive.

Save them, Lord!"

~297~

St. Ignatius of Loyola used to repeat a prayer that I love. With it on our lips and in our hearts, we will continue this narrow and rough path that leads us to God.

> "Take, Lord, and receive all my liberty,
> my memory, my understanding,
> and my entire will.
>
> You have given all to me; to you,
> Lord, I return it.
>
> Everything is yours;
> do with it according to your will.
>
> Give me only your love and your grace;
> that is enough for me."

~298~

Today is a special day. God is near. Can you experience His loving presence? It fills your soul with a sweet and boundless hope.

~299~

Every time a little spark jumps in my heart, the good God comes to blow on it and turn it into a blazing fire. From God comes serenity. Knowing that nothing will happen to us because He is with us. From God comes this love that envelops us and embraces the heart. It makes us cry with emotion... The Good God, all love and mercy. From God comes this immense joy that makes us want to share it. It's so much that it overflows. From God comes this tenderness that makes us want to embrace the sick, the hungry, the elderly, the brother, the lonely.

~300~

With you...

You only need God.
Cling to the Lord,
and you will emerge
victorious.

~301~

Sometimes you feel like you can't go on. It has happened to many. Anguish invades your body. It seems like there's nowhere to turn. Paths have closed before you. Suddenly, you find yourself with no options left. It is then that the Immense Power of God suddenly manifests itself. And you see Him in all His Glory.

You are like Moses facing the Red Sea. You have the entire people of Israel under your care, and behind you, an army ready to kill them. What to do? How did you end up in this situation? Moses trusts. He knows Whom he listens to. Who is there. He stretches out his hand and the sea opens before them. They pass through and are saved. God is waiting for that moment... for you to trust. Just take your first step. I guarantee you. He won't delay. He will come to you and embrace you and comfort you. I know. God dwells in you. He walks with you. You are not alone. I live it daily. It's not the same to read it as it is to live it. God must be experienced. Feel His presence. Know His Providence. Then you will understand as I did 23 years ago. With the experience of God, the world around you will change. You will know yourself as a child of the Most High. A child of God. A Prince. A Messenger. You hold in your hands a treasure, good news to share with the world.

"God exists. He is our Father and He loves us."

~302~

"The Eucharist is my highway to Heaven."
Blessed Carlo Acutis.

St. John Vianney used to say: "Put all the good works of the world against one Holy Mass; they will be as a grain of sand beside a mountain." If we truly understood the Mass, we would die of joy." And Padre Pio: "It would be easier for the world to survive without the sun than to do without the Mass." I try to attend daily Mass. I have found a Treasure and I want to share it with you. It is immense. It transcends. It goes beyond us. It is the presence of Jesus alive, in every Host consecrated by the hands of a priest. A tender and good Jesus. When I am in His presence, the world transforms for me. I look around and understand many things. That we are all brothers. That God loves us. That there is a purpose, a plan for each of us, that we are not here by chance. God in His infinite goodness wants you to be HAPPY. So many people talk about the elderly ladies who attend Mass every morning. If they only knew they are right. They found this Treasure and wouldn't trade it for anything. The presence of God. To be able to receive Him, to make Him part of our lives. Why do I tell you these things? Because I have realized... How many wonders the Lord has in store for us! It's phenomenal! There are no words! You must experience it. Live it... And everything will make sense.

~303~

Have you ever experienced this?

This morning, faced with a temptation, I thought: "If I lose grace, I will lose everything." And I realized how fragile we are, and how strong Jesus makes us when He is deep within us, in our hearts.

~304~

Sometimes, when I am about to complain about so many difficulties, it seems to me that Jesus, from that beautiful Tabernacle, says to me:

"Look at me, whenever you can, nailed to the cross. Without pain, there is no redemption."

It reminds me of these words I once read:

"It is better to be nailed with Jesus on the cross than to simply look at Him."

~305~

Believe me. My life has never been the same since the day I decided for God. I learned to trust in His love and to live by Divine Providence. I've been called a "weirdo" countless times. But I've been happy being misunderstood.

~306~

Come on, why are you so troubled? Even if it seems impossible, there is a way out, a path to discover. Just trust, pray with perseverance, surrender yourself into God's loving hands, and He will resolve it. I have seen it hundreds of times.

~307~

"God always gives us another chance."

~308~

In the end, life is about new beginnings. Made a mistake? It's okay. Start over.

~309~

I dreamed I was at Mass. I participated with great fervor. The priest's words, the Gospel, the consecration, all moved me deeply. The moment of communion arrived, and I asked our Lord:
— What hurts you the most about us?
And it seemed to me that dear Jesus, saddened, replied:
— It hurts me the indifference.
— Are we indifferent towards you? — I asked, puzzled.

Then my eyes were opened, as if a layer of mud fell from them, and I saw what I had never noticed before. The priest, holding the holy host, raised it so the faithful could see it and adore our Lord in their hearts.

— The body of Christ — he said.

— Amen — replied those receiving our Lord, but their thoughts were elsewhere, in another place, distant.

As this unfolded, I could see the people in the pews. In such a sacred moment, when Jesus himself becomes present for us, we did not know him. He was a stranger whom few greeted. Jesus looked at us with such great love, but we did not see him, nor did we pray or adore his body and blood. Many in their pews were chatting, others were reading the Catholic weekly, others were thinking about their businesses. And Jesus looked at them with sadness.

— Do you understand now? — he said to me.

I also felt great pain in my heart and soul. How could we not love you, Lord?

The next day I went to Mass and remembered this dream. On my knees, I asked our Lord to grant us all his love, so that we may love him more, with all our heart and soul.

That day, Mass took on a new meaning for me. Something had changed. I felt it more luminous, more spiritual, deeper. And I understood why they teach us that it is the perfect prayer, thanksgiving, the Eucharist.

~310~

You know, every day, when I visit Jesus in the Tabernacle after Mass, I ask him the same question: "What should I do?" I often can't find answers to my concerns and don't know how to solve my problems. Today was a special day, different.

I was in that solitary dialogue with Jesus. I asked him many things, certain that He is there, seeing me and listening to me. And suddenly these thoughts came to me. Since I didn't have paper to write them down, I wrote them on the palm of my hand. After leaving the Church, I came to the Library. Here I am now, reading what I wrote: "He who lives in the presence of God cannot hate, even if he wants to. God is Love. His love is so great that it floods everything and leaves no space in your soul for hatred, resentment, or bitterness. In His presence there is only peace, serenity, forgiveness, and mercy."

There is more. Looking steadfastly at Him, I reminded Him of the problems I'm going through and don't know how to solve. Then I felt a balm in my soul. "It's You," I said, "I know it's You." And a deep love filled me with such strength that even now, in this moment, in this place, I feel it. It's an indescribable inner joy. And it moves me to love everything, everyone, the good, the bad, those who love me, and those who hate me. At that moment, I asked again the question that had always gone unanswered:

"What should I do?" This time something happened. "What should I do?" I asked again. I felt an inner voice, clear as the wind, reaching my heart. "Love," it answered. "You must love."

Then I understood. I have loved, but not enough. I have loved with a very poor and selfish love, a selective love. I must take that first step that sets us apart and love a little more. Then, ask Him for a spark of His love, which is pure and clean, to love as I should love. As I left, I came to this conclusion: If we loved just a little more, the world would be different, and so would we.

Now you know. Every time you ask what you should do, you will find only one answer: "LOVE."

~311~

Do you lack peace? It's because you've been looking in the wrong place. We are called to be happy, but happiness cannot be found in anything of this world. Everything we possess is marked with "temporary."

True happiness, the lasting kind... Do you know how to find it? John Paul II told the youth in Toronto that the Beatitudes are like a map to happiness, and in them, you will find the face of Jesus.

I asked a friend who converted to Catholicism: — What must one do to find peace? He replied: — Find God.

Yes, it is possible to be happy. We are called to it. The answer is God. Look no further. There is no other answer.

In Italy, during World War II, a young girl named Chiara Lubich asked herself these questions. She saw how bombs were destroying everything people held dear—their homes, their possessions; lovers were separated, wives lost their husbands... There was a shortage of food and hope. In the midst of that turmoil, she thought: — Will there be something that truly endures? Something bombs cannot destroy? She concluded that there was. "It was God."

She gathered with some friends and decided to live the Gospel life with them. Loving, sharing, being one with all. The destruction of war did not discourage her; instead, it motivated her to do something to make the world better.

Unknowingly, she founded a movement in the Catholic Church: "the Focolare." Today, there are over four million Focolare members around the world, including priests, bishops, laypeople, and consecrated individuals.

What is Peace? Chiara says: "It is being with God. The one who has God in their heart has peace."

Love and trust have the power to transform us all. The Psalmist, who understood the condition of man and the greatness of God, transmitted this trust to us so that we too may trust: "I trust in God and have no fear." (Psalm 56) "I feel secure and have no fear, for Yahweh is my strength and my song, He is my salvation." (Isaiah 12:2)

It's not half-hearted trust or a passing illusion. It's something true, just as the ways of God are true. "You who dwell in the shelter of the Most High, who abide in the shadow of the Almighty, say to the Lord: 'My refuge, my fortress; my God, in whom I trust.'" (Psalm 91)

A friend recently told me: "When I'm in an airplane passing through clouds where nothing is visible, I always think of faith. If we trust our lives to the plane's instruments, can't we trust a Loving Father who seeks and gives us what is best for us, even if it's not what we desire most?"

~312~

Have you seen a group of children playing? They are pure. They have innocence in their souls and hearts. The tenderness of a child is priceless. I remember when my daughter Ana Belen, who is now a lawyer and writer, was just a few months old. I would come home tired from work in the evenings; as I opened the door, Vida, my wife, would start singing:

— Daddy's home.

Then a beautiful little lady would appear down the hallway, crawling towards me, excitedly, with a huge smile. I would pick her up, and with her little hands she would wrap around my neck and plant a kiss on my forehead. I never recovered from these greetings. They left me deeply moved. They were a gift from God. Years passed. One day at work, I searched in my pants pocket for a very important key and instead found a wooden toy horse. I smiled to myself.

— It must have been Ana Belen, — I thought happy.

From that day on, I started finding surprises in my pockets. Ana Belen, my little daughter, would place them there so that I would think of her all day... my sun, my moon, my star, my little princess. So many beautiful memories, surely you have them too. They help me to think of God's goodness and mercy. God is good. Trust in Him.

~313~

Do you suffer? I know, there is so much suffering around us. We don't understand why we must endure this endless pain. A close family member who has passed away, lack of love at home, many needs we cannot meet, feeling lonely and abandoned.

I remember an elderly lady I visited with a friend, to bring her communion. She was so weak she couldn't get out of her bed.

Once she said to me:
— See how much I suffer.
I responded with those supernatural words that Saint Josemaría Escrivá, as a young priest, whispered to a sick person after administering the sacrament of the sick:
— Blessed be the pain. Glorified be the pain.
And I explained to her the meaning of suffering offered to God. She became calm, serene. Taking my hand, she said to me:
— There is so much to offer.
— Indeed, there is, — I replied.

She closed her eyes and rested, meditating on her life, enduring the pain.

The truth is that God never abandons us. I am witness to how the lives of many around me have changed. They have learned to recognize that "God is alive, and He loves us." How can we not love Him? How can we not long to be in His presence?

A few days ago, a priest friend told me the story of a man who was diagnosed with terminal cancer. He was young, married, and had three young children. That day, he took his car and drove around, unable to contain his pain and anguish, while he cried out to God: "Why me? Why me?" He cried bitterly, unable to hold back. Suddenly, he felt a sweet presence, like a gentle breeze surrounding him, and he heard clearly as daylight, a kind voice saying to him: "Do not be afraid. I am with you." From that moment on, he faced his illness with serenity, offering his fears and sufferings for the conversion of poor sinners. God always accompanies us, never leaves us alone. He takes care of us and invites us to be holy to live eternity in the promised Paradise. I remember a time when I complained to Him.

Lord: You have me in your loving presence. I have come to see you and talk to you. I still don't find answers to my concerns. Who are you? Who am I? What do you desire from me? How can I find you? Why suffering? Why do I sometimes feel I can't go on? There is so much I wish to know.

My child: If you only knew how much I love you. If you had a little faith. If you dared to trust in my plans. If you sought me more often. Then, your life would change. You would be immensely happy.

~314~

We have lost the purity of heart, that's why we are exposed to so many dangers.

~315~

"You are the Queen of the universe and I want to be your subject." Saint Alphonsus to the Virgin Mary.

Can I give you advice? It's simple and very practical. In the midst of your difficulties, turn to Mary. A few years ago, I read a news story that didn't receive much attention: "Miraculous Medal saves executive." It was surprising to find this story in a newspaper that generally does not publish religious reviews. I still remember what it said about that businessman who was having lunch with his friends in a restaurant. A hitman on a motorcycle passed by and started firing his machine gun at them. Chaos reigned. Broken glasses, scattered glass, blood, and three motionless bodies on the floor. Suddenly, one of them gets up. Very sore, he checks himself for wounds. He feels something round and hard on his chest. It didn't take him long to realize what had happened. The bullet meant to kill him was embedded in his Miraculous Medal. He was the only survivor of this attack. I've been taught since I was little that when sin prevents you from approaching Jesus, we have Mary to intercede for us. Since we were children, my mother has told my brothers and me: "You have a Mother in heaven." You might ask me:

— So much trust placed in Mary? ...

— How could I not? She is my mother!

Through the years, I've experienced her maternal protection. And I know that right now she also intercedes for your needs and those of your family. It's always easier to approach a mother. We are not worthy of grace, but Mary's love leads us to her son, by short and safe paths. Since I was a child, I've felt her very close, like mothers are, close and attentive to their children. She is a beautiful mother. And she always keeps her promises.

On my chest hangs a Franciscan cross and a Miraculous Medal. It is the only medal sent down from heaven. The Virgin showed it to Saint Catherine Labouré. The Virgin promised Saint Catherine: "Those who wear it will receive great graces, especially if they wear it around their neck with confidence." So many miracles happened because of this medal that people called it the "Miraculous Medal."

A family was returning to the city on the Interamerican Highway. They had a small baby, just a few months old. Suddenly, a speeding truck veered into their lane and hit them head-on. The crash was terrible. Pieces of twisted metal were left from the car. It was a horrible collision. That evening, another family was watching the sunset, sitting on the porch of their house. They were involuntary witnesses and testified to what happened. At the moment of impact, the baby was thrown out, through the windshield, and flew toward large, sharp rocks without any resistance. Suddenly, out of nowhere, he stopped. It was as if someone had held him in the air. Literally, he was floating, Then he gently descended to settle on a small mound of grass. The laws of physics are immutable. Those who witnessed the accident could not understand or explain the obvious miracle. His mother could understand it. I was at her house and she told me the secret, showing me the little one sleeping peacefully in his crib. She had consecrated him to the Virgin and always had a little miraculous medal on him. In my family, the Virgin has always remained present. She is part of us, like our children and grandparents. We experience her maternal protection in the most difficult moments of life. We are confident in knowing that she is near, with us. I can't remember a single occasion when I was distressed and approached the Virgin Mary and she didn't listen to me. I love this ejaculation in which we invoke her protection. And I try to repeat it whenever I can: "Oh Mary, conceived without sin, pray for us who have recourse to you." Turning to the Virgin is the secret that the saints have transmitted to us. It is the shortest path to reach Jesus. A journey without major mishaps. It gives us the certainty of being able to save our souls, not by our own merits, which are few, but by her intercession as a mother before her son Jesus... I wear a Miraculous Medal, and every morning I thank the Virgin for her maternal protection. How good Mary is, as she protects us from the dangers and snares of the enemy of souls. It's no wonder they call her "Mary Help of Christians." I like to call her: "Helper."

~316~

I remember one day in a department store seeing something curious. The gardening manager was arranging some cans. Then he stopped and I saw him mumbling a few words with his eyes closed. Another salesperson saw me watching and approached me:

—He's praying —he said quietly—. He does it every hour.

I approached with curiosity and asked him:

—What are you doing?

—I'm saying a Hail Mary —he said simply—. It's how I greet the Virgin.

Sister María Romero, like many saints, reflected on this same theme and wrote in her diary:

Who is Mary?

1. My Queen.
2. My celestial Princess.
3. My delight of Paradise and Jesus's delight.
4. The beloved Mother of Jesus.
5. My treasure of Jesus.

And then she asks: Who is she that by loving her I give Jesus the greatest proof of love? Who is the oasis of the Heart of Jesus and mine? Who is my arrow of love to reach Jesus? What is the celestial instrument to sing my love to Jesus? The answer is only one and she writes it next: Mary!

~317~

I wanted to let you know that you will never find Peace if you remain chained to sin, to your fears, to gossip, to negative thoughts, to hatred, to resentment, and if you do not live the fullness of your faith. A woman of faith trusts in God, knows He is a father who cares for her, and believes that nothing bad will happen to her.

Peace is found in the freedom that the children of God have. More than a feeling, it is a reality that allows them to love those who do not love them back, that helps them trust in God in times of difficulty, that makes them shine like a star on the horizon. They are the salt of the earth, and their light shines before men.

We must regain trust in God who is Almighty. Proclaim our faith without fear. Being a woman of faith grants you many privileges. God spoils you abundantly. I have seen it and know what I am talking about. A friend wrote me an email telling me about his experience: 'In my country, we are ashamed Catholics. We are embarrassed to openly practice our religion. We have bad examples from our parents (not from our mothers) who want nothing to do with religion until they are dying. Then they want a priest to come. And sometimes, not even then. I was just in a hospital visiting a friend, and the neighbor in the next bed did not want to confess. I told him he needed more courage to return to God than to sin... the next day he did.'

~318~

There was a time in my life when I supported my parish priest as an Extraordinary Minister of Holy Communion. I used to bring communion to a cousin who was very ill with cancer. Since she could barely swallow, I would give her tiny pieces of the Holy Host. We prayed and marveled at this great Gift: the presence of Jesus. One afternoon, I went with Jesus to visit her. She could no longer swallow. The disease had progressed, and she was receiving morphine for terrible pain. But when Jesus arrived, it seemed like a transformation occurred. That day, I set up a small table and placed the pyx containing the Blessed Sacrament on it. We spent some time in Adoration. I remembered then the story a friend, who is a priest, told me. He lives in Mexico. His family is Jewish, and he converted to Catholicism over the years. He told me that once he was with a bishop and they entered a chapel. The Blessed Sacrament was exposed, and the bishop knelt down in devotion and prayed silently. My friend, puzzled, didn't yet understand what was happening and asked the bishop: —Why are you kneeling?

The bishop pointed to the altar, where the monstrance with the Blessed Sacrament was placed.

—That Host you see there is Jesus. He sees you and hears you. I approached my cousin, who could barely move her eyes due to weakness. I opened the pyx to expose the Holy Host.

—This is Jesus —I told her—. He sees you and hears you. Suddenly, she began to lift her head and body, with a difficulty you cannot imagine. Nothing seemed to stop her. She wanted to see Jesus. With her body slightly raised, she stared at the white Host, with the wonder of a child seeing something marvelous for the first time. Then she collapsed back onto the bed, exhausted. I closed my pyx and handed it to her.

—Jesus wants to embrace you —I said—. Embrace Him too. She took the closed pyx in her worn hands and pressed it tightly against her chest. She closed her eyes and bowed her head. It was a striking moment of silence and profound prayer, born from the soul itself, that impressed all of us who were present in that room. Minutes passed. She clung to the loving embrace of Jesus. One of her daughters approached and said to her:

—Mom, mom... And gently, she took the pyx from her and handed it to me. I asked if anyone in the room was prepared to receive Communion. The daughter indicated:

—I can, and I would like to receive.

I gave her Communion, and she embraced her sick mother with emotion.

—You have just received Holy Communion —I told her—. Right now, you are a living Tabernacle. By embracing your mother, Jesus is also embracing her.

That day, I left that house moved and happy. As I got into the car, I stopped for a moment to pray and ended up acknowledging:

—How good you are, Jesus!"

~319~

"Let a pleasant fragrance be spread like incense, let their flowers bloom like the lily, give off their perfume, and sing praise. Bless the Lord for all his works!" Sirach 39:14

Recently, a friend reminded me that we should live in the presence of God, and that ejaculatory prayers help us achieve this. I once read that an ejaculation is like an arrow of love that we launch into the heart of God, and at the same time, it brings us peace and tranquility. They can be repeated throughout the day, while driving, at work, or at home. They are very short prayers and an expression of love, directed to God, Jesus, His Mother, or good St. Joseph. Here are some that I frequently use:

"Sacred Heart of Jesus, I trust in You." "Sweet Heart of Mary, be my salvation." "Jesus, Joseph, and Mary, I give you my heart and soul."

Is there one in particular that you like to repeat to keep the presence of God in your day? Give it a try and write to me about how it goes. I'll leave my contact information at the end of the book. God is good.

~320~

"I have said these things to you, that in me you may have peace." John 16:33

And where is the peace that I seek, Claudio? Peace is a gift, a grace that must be sought. But first, you must believe. Have faith. Trust in God. True peace does not come from this world. Jesus clarified it, saying: "Peace I leave with you; my peace I give to you. Not as the world gives do I give to you. Let not your hearts be troubled, neither let them be afraid." John 14:27 There is no recipe you can use to find that peace. That's why some people are led astray by wrong paths. They think that happiness found in life's pleasures will eventually become enduring. This has never happened. Power, greed, lust, money, alcohol, drugs, reckless living, and bitterness have only served to drown them in their own despair. It's like falling into a dark tunnel and instead of climbing out to the surface, they start digging deeper, sinking further down. They do not know that Christ passes by and heals their lives. They do not know God. Nor have they experienced the tenderness of the Father.

Do you think no one loves you? God does love you. And He loves you madly, like no one else has been able to, nor will be able to. And He says to console you: "Can a woman forget her nursing child, or show no compassion for the child of her womb? Even these may forget, yet I will not forget you." (Isaiah 49:15)

I spoke with some friends who went through a very tough situation. They were in the midst of the storm for nearly two years until they emerged from it, strengthened, happy, and secure in their relationship with God. I asked them what they did. Here was their response:

- They acknowledged they had a problem. They sought professional help and spiritual guidance.
- They placed the problem in God's hands and committed to seeking Him, surrendering their lives completely to Him, and humbly and confidently asking for His mercy.
- They engaged in activities that helped them distract themselves, clear their minds, so they weren't constantly dwelling on the problem.
- They examined their consciences, sought a priest, and confessed, so they could devoutly participate in Holy Mass and receive Communion worthily.

One of them commented: "No one can give you the peace that comes from confessing to a priest. After absolution, you feel renewed. Inside you, you exclaim: What relief! Because you have lifted a heavy burden." They discovered that Jesus holds the key to everything. Only He can calm the storms that rock our lives and restore Peace.

~321~

Today I will share with you some good advice. It was given to me by a priest I used to confess to:

'Do all the good you can. Let it be said of you: He passed through the world, doing good.'

~322~

When you live in the presence of God, everything has a purpose, even if you don't understand it at first. It's like weaving an intricate tapestry without knowing exactly what you're doing or what the final result will be. There comes a moment when you stop questioning and simply continue your life knowing that you live in God and that He guides your steps. It is then that you realize God's reasons, and that everything has been for good. Sometimes, all it takes is trust… Give it a try. Trust. God will do the rest. Come on. 'Trust in the Lord and do good; dwell in the land and enjoy safe pasture. Take delight in the Lord, and he will give you the desires of your heart. Commit your way to the Lord; trust in him and he will do this: He will make your righteous reward shine like the dawn, your vindication like the noonday sun.' (Psalm 37:3-6) You don't have to wait for a big difficulty to turn your gaze to heaven; any day is a good day to start. If you do, you'll rediscover the taste for prayer and, incidentally, you'll be saving your soul. My experience is similar to that of the psalmist (Psalm 25) when he wrote: 'No one who hopes in you will ever be put to shame.' I have never been disappointed by God, although I have disappointed Him. Just today at Mass, they read a psalm. I sat down and started listening: 'No one who hopes in you will ever be put to shame.' 'Wow,' I thought, 'that's exactly what I just wrote.' I smiled, thinking, 'How good you are, Lord.'

Trusting in God, seeking Him, is something wonderful that you must live and experience.

~323~

What have I learned over these years?

That what they have told us is true.
Whoever dwells in the presence of God
is happy.

~324~

God wants you to be good. And then to be holy. Our time is so short. Be as holy as you can be. Never forget that you were created for eternity.

~325~

"After their prayer, the place where they were gathered shook, and they were all filled with the Holy Spirit and spoke the word of God boldly." Acts 4:31

Discovering that God's love changes your life. You'll never be the same. God is wonderful; knowing Him has been the best thing that happened to me. You learn to live by Providence and accept everything as coming from His loving hands. One thing is hearing about God, and another is experiencing His presence in your life. Just yesterday, after Mass, a young woman approached me with some questions. She was restless, overflowing with joy.

"I can tell you've had an encounter with God," I said. "How do you know?"

"From your enthusiasm. You're happy. A sign of God's presence is joy. Look at children they're pure, full of God, and always joyful."

"That's true," she replied.

"But I still haven't fully grasped what happened to me. Can I tell you?"

"Of course," I said. "I used to live every moment intensely parties, my dream job, a new car, nothing worried me but something was missing. I wasn't happy. A few weeks ago, I had a dream. It was intense. I was in God's presence, and He showed me who I really am—not who I thought I was or who others imagined me to be. I saw myself almost transparent, as He sees me, unable to hide the smallest sin, everything laid bare before me. A foul-smelling, dark stain enveloped and chained me. In that moment, before God, I couldn't lie or justify those deeds. I understood the magnitude of my sins and how they offended God—horrible sins I committed knowingly, without remorse, out of pride and desire. It was an overwhelming and terrifying experience. I felt deep repentance, an almost perfect contrition, like never before. I understood I needed to change and seek God. I was convinced He forgave me and gave me a new chance. There was still time. He had a wonderful plan for me. And I let Him know I was ready to discover it. When I woke up, everything looked different. I didn't want to be the same. Something had changed inside me."

"And that joy you carry within?"

"I don't know. It's something I can't explain. I feel a love overflowing within me. I feel a desire to forgive everything and everyone. I want to embrace anyone in front of me, tell them God loves them, that He is our Father. I don't care what others think, only what God thinks and wants from me. I want Him to be pleased with my actions, thoughts, and words. Honestly, it's madness. But I'm happy. I don't know what's happening to me. I want to know more about God, read the Bible, live for Him, have moments of intimacy and silence in His presence, away from the world, in some solitary place. God and I. Nothing else."

"It's the joy of the presence of the Holy Spirit," I said. "God is wooing you. He fills you with His grace. And along the way, He'll show you what He desires of you. Don't worry about that for now. Just enjoy this unrepeatable moment, unique in which you'll live by grace and His love."

"And what will happen next?"

"You'll need to strengthen your faith because you'll live by it. How? Through daily Mass, frequent confession, fervent prayer, reading the Word of God and Catholic books on spirituality. Fight to keep the grace. That's what a woman of faith does. God will help you."

"How will my life be?"

"It will be wonderful. A great adventure. First, we live by grace; then, we live by faith. Imagine a father holding his little one to help him start walking. That's grace. And then he says, 'Now you have to do it on your own. Come on, you can do it.' And he lets go. That's faith. We dare to go joyfully into the world, carrying His love, trusting blindly, knowing He goes with us."

"And what does God want from me?"

"For now, He wants you to love Him. And love your neighbor."

"And what else?"

"To recognize your mistakes and believe in His Mercy; to start over again and again. Because the most important thing isn't falling but getting up and moving forward. As a priest once said, 'A saint isn't someone who never falls, but someone who always gets up.'"

"And if what I'm doing is bearing fruit and I don't see it?"

"Don't worry about that because the fruit will be seen at harvest time. When a farmer sows wheat, he doesn't wonder if the grain is suffering its transformative process; rather, he pays attention to each stage of growth, to provide whatever is lacking. Don't worry about the weeds in the field."

"In your daily life, God wants simplicity, to live your faith naturally and joyfully, to praise Him, and love Him; to never forget to visit Him in the Tabernacle, to share Him with everyone you know or don't; to speak of how good and wonderful He is to you, how He protects, indulges, instructs, guides you... and how He claims your love, His Love."

"He wants you to be His daughter.
To have faith.
To not lose hope.
To trust in Him.
To endure everything with patience,
temperance, and fortitude.
To have mercy.
To offer everything for His Love.
To fight for your ideals and values.
To be a reflection of Him in life.
And to bring Him to others.

~326~

"And God is able to make all grace abound to you, so that in all things, at all times, having all that you need, you will abound in every good work." 2 Corinthians 9:8

There are two important truths you must know:

1. God loves you. He is Almighty. With Him by your side, nothing bad will happen to you.
2. One of the devil's favorite weapons is to take away our peace. He knows that fear paralyzes us. He knows that if we live in anguish, we will stop working for the Kingdom, drift away from prayer, and turn our backs on God.

People who live in this way, with fears, spend their days bitterly and ask: "Why me?" They don't make time for prayer, they lose their trust and spiritual life. Life is a gift from God and we must use it to do good and bear abundant fruit. If we don't change, we will be judged at the end of times for our lack of faith, for being too selfish, for our lack of love. We've been told everything, but we pay little attention. The devil strives to make us fall without mercy, filling us with doubts, fears, and worldly desires. We forget the power of faith and trust in the Heavenly Father, and that's why we sink into despair.

I'm sure you've noticed this: "People who love spend their days in peace, with inner joy, immersed in eternal Love, ready to serve others, and to bring this immense treasure to those in need. They are recognized by their fruits and... 'the fruit of the Spirit is love, joy, peace, patience, kindness, goodness, faithfulness, gentleness, self-control...' (Galatians 5:22-23)

A concrete example of our times is Mother Teresa of Calcutta. Have you ever heard her complain? She spent her life serving God and the needy. She lived in the Father's Love, pouring out this love abundantly; and she did so until her last breath.

A good way to overcome fears is to stop thinking about ourselves and start thinking about others. I see it while driving. Almost no one lets you cross from one side of the street to the other anymore. Desperate to get there first, they throw their car at you. However, there's always someone who stops with a kind smile and signals for you to go ahead. In their face, you can see Peace and serenity.

Once I asked a committed person in the Church who I always saw joyful, helpful, and serene:

—How do you know when something comes from God?

—Because it gives you peace.

Yes, my friend, to find Peace, you must find God. Peace. Peace. Peace.

May the peace of the good God dwell in your heart.

Do you feel better? Now, dedicate time to prayer, to thank the Father for the gifts with which He blesses you daily, to ask for His favors, and to help build a better world.

Start a new path now, without selfishness, with a pure soul, as disciples of Jesus, with a new purpose in life and enthusiasm, with joy and great joy in your heart. Come on, what are you waiting for! Your brother needs you. There is much to do, a whole world to evangelize.

"Go into all the world and preach the gospel..." Mark 16:15

~327~

Advice from the Bible

Do you want to succeed? There's a very simple formula. And it's biblical.

"Commit to the Lord whatever you do, and he will establish your plans."

Proverbs 16:3

~328~

"When the voices and experiences of women are heard, society is deeply enriched. Let us pray together that, through encounter and dialogue, the 'feminine genius' may flourish in today's world." Pope Francis

I want to talk to you today about my wife Vida, dedicating this day to that wonderful woman who accompanies me and loves me. Does that sound good to you? She doesn't know I'm writing these words, I want them to be a gift, a way to honor her. Her name is Vida, like life. We've been married for 39 years, have 4 children and a beautiful granddaughter, Ana Sofía. It's been an adventure sharing my life with Vida. She's joyful, talkative, and has a unique sense of belonging. She perceives things that I don't see, as if she has X-ray vision. Over the years, she's come to know my virtues and flaws better than anyone else. She's cultivated great patience. She can discern what my gestures, looks, and even thoughts conceal. I might head downstairs wanting a coffee to share a moment with her, and before I finish descending the stairs she says, 'I'll make you coffee, and I'm sure you're here for one.' It's the same with our children; they can't hide anything from her. For me, this ability of women, mothers, and wives is a mystery. In jest, I tell her, 'Woman, let me think, give me a chance to speak.' We like to go on Thursdays to a chapel with the Blessed Sacrament and spend time with Jesus, thanking Him for so many blessings, care, and love. We pray, entrust our dreams to Him, and pray for our family and yours too. You hold this book in your hands thanks to her. Surely you read the reason on one of the first pages of the Devotional. I was about to turn 50, feeling restless. I had so many questions and was praying. 'What will I do with the rest of my life?' I wondered. One afternoon Vida approached me, hugged me, and said, *'You have a dream and it's time to fulfill it. Quit your job, everything you do, and dedicate yourself to writing. God will help you, we will get through this, and you will do what you love.'* I did as she said. And at first, things went very badly. We were on the verge of losing our house due to missed mortgage payments. But God intervened, I learned to trust, and everything improved. That's an amazing story for another book where I'll tell you what it's like to live on Divine Providence, when God provides for your material and spiritual needs, and you lack nothing, no matter how incredible it may seem. It all boils down to trust.

If you trust a lot, you receive a lot.
If you trust a little, you receive a little.

This writer's profession is curious; sometimes I meet a reader in a pharmacy, a store, a church; they approach me, but not to me, to Vida: 'You're Vida, Mr. Claudio's wife, right?' Another time in a bakery, the shopkeeper brings me a package of meringues. 'Take them, your wife loves them and always buys them.' I enjoy my married life, Proverbs 31 says: '*A woman of character, where can she be found? She is far more precious than jewels. Her husband trusts her with no lack of gain. She brings him good, not harm, all the days of her life*.' And I have found this to be true; it describes my wife perfectly. I love you, Vida.

Over the years, I've learned that women have extraordinary abilities and gifts that men don't even dream of, and that woman is the perfect complement to man, and man to woman. On their 50th wedding anniversary, my wife's mother said these words: '*Sometimes I look back and realize that without God, we couldn't have made it*.'

God is good. He has given me a good woman as a companion on the journey. Together we will travel the path of life until He, in His infinite wisdom, decides otherwise.

Thank you, Lord!

~329~

"With him we have the certainty that if we ask anything according to his will, he hears us." 1 John 5:14

Are you doubting? Are you mistrusting God?

It's time to start trusting and reclaim your life to be happy. You need answers. Let's see what the Bible, the Word of God, tells us, where everything written there comes true. Do you have one handy? Open it and read:

"Blessed is the one who trusts in the Lord, whose confidence is in him. They will be like a tree planted by the water that sends out its roots by the stream. It does not fear when heat comes; its leaves are always green. It has no worries in a year of drought and never fails to bear fruit." Jeremiah 17:7-8

"Commit your way to the Lord; trust in him and he will do this: He will make your righteous reward shine like the dawn, your vindication like the noonday sun." Psalm 37:5-6

Are there still reasons to doubt? I don't think so. Put it to the test. God always keeps his word.

~330~

I think I've mentioned this throughout this devotional. Jesus has always been my neighbor. When I was a child, we lived across from the Servants of Mary. They had a small, beautiful chapel. I loved crossing the street to visit Jesus. It filled me with joy to see him because he was my best friend. I remember asking him many things. I realize that I haven't changed much. I still ask him, full of questions. Now, as an adult, for a time I lived across from a student residence. I used to say that Jesus was my neighbor because they have a quiet oratory that invites prayer. Jesus is always there, in the tabernacle. At night, I sometimes think about the great grace of having him as a neighbor. I peek out the window and greet him. He loves these little gestures and smiles.

Recently, I felt compelled to ask him: "What do you do in the tabernacle? I can move freely wherever I want, but you are like a prisoner, exposed to being moved from one place to another, waiting for someone to visit you. During this time, what do you do? What are you dedicated to?"

In the afternoon, I went to Mass and asked again. It seemed to me he replied: "Why do I have to do something? Loving is enough for me. You are always in a hurry to go from one place to another, but do you love? You have forgotten the most important thing."

After Mass, I went to see my friend Father Angel. I know he loves talking about Jesus, so I told him about my concern. It seems to me that Jesus wants to teach us something in the tabernacle, I said. And visibly pleased, he replied, "We must learn the virtues of Jesus in the Eucharist." He also said something that I liked very much: "Jesus becomes poor, vulnerable, because he loves us." This is something that has always amazed me. Jesus is there, exposed to everything, our love or our indifference. I found some answers to my question. Jesus in the tabernacle teaches us these virtues:

- Patience.
- Humility.
- Love.
- Trust.
- Silence.
- Serenity.
- Obedience.

Everything about Jesus surprises me. We talk so much that we have forgotten how pleasant it is to gather in silence to meditate on the wonders of the Lord. His silence is an invitation to prayer. His patience, to be patient. His humility, to be humble. His trust, to trust. I have come to this conclusion: What does Jesus do while he waits for us? He loves. He burns with love for humanity, for us; and he asks the Father to bless us and fill us with graces.

~331~

You have just left the confessional. You have encountered the Mercy of God. You make the resolution to not offend Him again. You ask for strength and abundant graces to continue through life in a state of grace. It's such great joy. So incomparable.

This morning I went to confession. I feel happy. I wish you could also experience this immense joy that springs from the soul.

I have been able to go to the Tabernacle and look Jesus in the eyes. What peace. So much that it spreads around you.

You have the certainty that all your sins have been forgiven and that God has forgotten them. That's why I stop thinking about them and think about God's call instead.

What a wonderful certainty. You know that God dwells in you again and you in Him. This extraordinary promise of Jesus reminds me: "If you remain in me and my words remain in you, ask whatever you wish, and it will be done for you" (John 15:7).

I feel that I have returned to living in His love and that my heart is once again a living Tabernacle. I would like to always remain in His love and bear abundant fruits.

I eagerly await tomorrow to go to Mass and receive communion.

Before confessing, I thought: "If one of my children came to me after doing something silly and asked for forgiveness, I would surely say to them, 'Before you did that silly thing, I had already forgiven you.' If I, imperfect as I am, am like this, how much more can I expect from God, who is all love?"

How terrible it is to live with sin weighing on your shoulders. It's like being submerged in a dark and silent pit, with no hope of ever getting out. You live risking your greatest gift: "a wonderful eternity beside God."

It's not worth walking like that. It's better to approach God, like the prodigal son, and ask for forgiveness, to approach the confessional and renew our friendship with the Eternal Father.

Cheer up! I invite you to feel what I feel and to live what I am living now: Peace, serenity, and a joy so great and true that I would like to carry it with me always. Go to confession, renew your life as a beloved daughter and woman of God.

~332~

Do you have difficulties? Don't know what to do? Do you feel like there's no way out of that pit?

I pray for you.

Everything will be alright.

~333~

Years ago, I decided to write down in a notebook the important words that give meaning to my life. Over time, I've collected some that are quite charming, others more serious. But I wrote them all with the hope and longing to become better. For some reason, I thought it would be good to share them with you today.

1. God.
2. Sweet will of God.
3. Perfection of works.
4. Soul in sanctifying grace.
5. Read the Bible.
6. Live the faith.
7. See Christ in the poor.
8. Longing for Paradise.
9. Lead a life pleasing to God.
10. Frequent the sacraments.
11. Forgive from the heart.
12. Live the sacraments.
13. Give thanks to God.
14. Desire what God wants.
15. Love God.
16. Be a friend of Jesus.
17. Love the Church.
18. Strive to be holy.
19. Daily communion.

~334~

Have you seen the sweet gaze of Jesus?

There's something in it that: questions you,
speaks to you,
embraces you,
floods you with love and tenderness,
unsettles you,
shows you who you are,
penetrates your soul, reveals how much he suffers,
cries out to you: "I thirst",
asks you: do you love me?,
and answers you: "I am, and I love you".

~335~

"Listen in silence, because if your heart is filled with other things, you cannot hear His voice." Mother Teresa of Calcutta

Years pass by, leaving behind wonderful memories. When my son Luis Felipe was 4 years old, we used to play a game of silence. We would go to a nearby park and close our eyes for a few seconds, just to discover the sounds around us. The whistling of the wind. Birds chirping. People playing with their children, joyfully laughing. A dog barking. A worker hammering at a nearby construction site. The one who discovered the most sounds would win the game. Years have gone by, and I still visit that park to be silent. What I enjoy most about silence is prayer. Discovering God's presence. Hearing His sweet voice kindly respond, "Here I am, with you." It fills me with a peace and serenity that accompany me throughout the day. Be silent. And listen. Jesus wants to speak to you.

~336~

"To love others not because they are good, but to make them good." Blessed Sister María Romero

When you look around, you understand that you are not alone. Others have felt this soulful restlessness that leads them back to God. They are living amazing experiences and wouldn't trade them for anything or anyone else.

~337~

Today I had an extraordinary experience and I wanted to share it with you. While driving, I stopped at a traffic light. A very poor man who was limping approached my car. He extended his hand, but I did not roll down the window. I watched him walk away with difficulty, and I remembered the words of Saint Alberto Hurtado: "The poor person is Christ." At that moment, I looked at him again, filled with regret for not helping him, and it seemed to me that I saw Christ himself walking away from me, carrying a very heavy cross.

I recalled a friend who used to attend Sunday Mass and would hide from the poor so they wouldn't ask him for alms. He sneaked in and even planned his exit to avoid being bothered, as the church atrium was filled with homeless people.

After receiving communion, something happened to him... that changed him. He stood behind a pillar, opened his prayer book, and came face to face with this Psalm (40) that corrected his indifference:

"Blessed is the one who is concerned for the poor and needy; in the day of trouble the Lord delivers him. The Lord protects and preserves him; he is called blessed in the land."

~338~

Tobit 12:9 "Almsgiving delivers from death, and it will purge away every sin. Those who perform deeds of charity and of righteousness will have fulness of life."

- **Story about Salustiano Pantoja**

"Salustiano Pantoja is a beggar whom I met asking for alms one Sunday afternoon at the Church of San Francisco in the city of San Salvador de Jujuy. Upon leaving Mass and passing through the inner doors of the church atrium, I saw this beggar, Salustiano, about three meters away. Immediately, I knew he would ask for alms. Faced with that, I stopped, lowered my gaze, and asked myself that question we all ask ourselves many times in the streets of Buenos Aires: Do I give or not? Still with my gaze lowered, I decided to give him a few coins so that he wouldn't get used to begging. I chose the coins and, when I raised my gaze, Salustiano was no longer in his place. I looked for the beggar and only found him when I looked inside the church. My surprise, incredulity, and joy could not have been greater: there was a person with their back turned, Salustiano, who was placing his coins in the church's collection box, that is, he was donating part of the alms that he, humbly, as a beggar, had received from us wealthy parishioners. Being part of a non-profit foundation, we often wonder how much economically a person should contribute to charitable works. After much exchange of ideas, also taking into account other societies, we estimate that it is expected that a committed and compassionate person donate between two to three percent of their total income. At this point, I think it is convenient that we do not start with the question of whether it is before taxes or only on profits, etc. Let it be clear: total income. Moreover, if we have surplus, we can increase the percentage until it hurts. Salustiano not only left me happy and educated, but also intrigued. Fifteen days later, I had to return to Jujuy and went to talk to him. I found him at the same church door, gave him a small alms, to which he thanked me again with a 'God bless you, sir.' I started a long conversation with him in which I told him that I participated in an institution where we worked with needy people, helping them improve their homes, and that to raise funds we did the same as him, asking those who have more. I also told him that we often doubted how much we could ask of a generous person. The conversation was long and gave me the opportunity to tell him, without offending him, about the joy he had given me a few days earlier when I found him giving his alms. That's when I dared to ask him how much he gave to the Church, to which he smiled and replied, 'If I receive 2 at the end of Mass, I give 1; if I receive 3, I give 1.50; if I receive 5, I give 2; and if I receive 6, which is very rare, I give 2.50.' He added, 'It's a way of giving back to God what He gives me.'

This story was not told to me; I saw it and lived it. Thank you, Salustiano." (José Luis Mendizábal).

P.S.: Salustiano is 74 years old, suffers from arthritis in his knees, does not drink, his wife is disabled, and he currently begs for alms "because the sale of flowers he used to do in the cemetery is very tough now."

When I first read Salustiano's story, I was deeply moved and ashamed. I saw myself taking some coins out of my pants pocket and counting them before depositing them in the Church.

So much has God given me! And I give Him crumbs in return! That is why I decided to change, to be generous, as God has been with me.

~339~

Life is not easy. You can't imagine how much everything costs me. Understanding God's will. Striving to be good, and then struggling to be holy. This is beyond my strength. Only the grace of God has allowed me to continue. As Jesus said: "Apart from me you can do nothing." And I can do nothing without Him.

Recently, I faced a great difficulty. Instead of becoming anxious, filled with fear, and questioning God with foolish questions, for some reason, perhaps pure grace, I surrendered myself into His arms. "Thy will be done," I said to Him. "Is God asking something of me?" I thought. Later, calmer, I asked Him: "Lord, what do you want me to do?" And I began to write and publish my books about the relationship I have with the good God, and the lives of many others who work, suffer, laugh, have families, and have told me their experiences. I encounter so many people around us who strive to live in the presence of God. And they have wonderful adventures with Him.

God has taught us that everything He has said is true. That His promises are fulfilled. And there is no reason to fear. There are some words that have always motivated me. Pope Benedict XVI said them: "Whoever lives in God's hands, always falls into God's hands." You begin to trust, and your life changes. God takes care of leading you along the paths He wants you to walk with Him. And He does it gently, so that you go without fear.

It's something I love about God. He knows our weaknesses. He knows that we are made of flesh and filled with worries. That's why He fills us with gifts and gives everything abundantly. He carries you in His hands as a loving Father and envelops you in His love.

What does God ask in return? Something so simple that it seems small: our love. That we love Him and also love our neighbors. That we be a living reflection of His love. When you begin to experience providence, you understand that it is an extraordinary Treasure. That's why I share it with you. It's worth it for you to live this experience. Holy abandonment. "God wants it, so do I."

To trust and abandon oneself in the hands of God. This is perfect joy: "Accepting His holy will. Knowing that God is our Father and takes care of us."

~340~

Some years ago, I made a decision that would change my life. "I will trust in God," I told myself, "despite everything. I will believe in His promises."

God knows how to show us His ways, almost always unexpectedly. He calls you little by little, filling you with gifts, showing you His Mercy. So many times, I did not know how to recognize His loving presence. And now, as I reflect on it, I discover Him even in the smallest things, the everyday, what goes unnoticed. God calls us to turn our gaze to heaven. We must feel yearnings for eternity.

I live new experiences that I never imagined before. And I am filled with emotion when I think of the good God, our Father, and His infinite love.

I spend my days writing about my experiences with the good God and those of many who share them with me, excited about this great discovery: "God is our Father and loves us immensely." I publish my books on Amazon where I share these wonderful experiences. And the good God has allowed me to dedicate myself to Him and my family completely. It is surprising. I have lacked nothing.

I discover Providence in surprising ways. This is a treasure. And I tell myself, "How did I not discover this before?" Between the world and God, I choose God. Between the temporal and the eternal, I choose eternity.

~341~

Do you live in fear? I have an urgent message for you, and it's biblical: Read carefully.

"Do not fear, for I am with you; do not be dismayed, for I am your God. I will strengthen you, I will help you, yes, I will uphold you with My righteous right hand." Isaiah 41:10

Now you know, God is with you, He hears you, He indulges you, He loves you, you are not alone. There is no reason to fear.

~342~

Saint John Chrysostom was one of the great doctors of the Church. He wrote these wonderful words about the Eucharist: "The blood of Christ renews in us the image of our King, produces an indescribable beauty, and does not allow the nobility of our souls to be destroyed, but irrigates and nourishes them."

But there are some truly extraordinary writings of his that have always impacted me, not because of the content of his words, but because of the certainty, faith, and serenity with which this saint declares his trust in Jesus. Let me share them with you.

He was an old man when he was sent into an unjust exile. He stood up upon hearing the sentence and said calmly:

"Christ is with me, what can I fear?... He has guaranteed me His protection. It is not in my own strength that I rely. I hold in my hands His written word. This is my staff, this is my security, this is my peaceful harbor. Even if the whole world is thrown into confusion, I read this written word that I carry with me, for it is my wall and my defense. What does it tell me? I am with you always, even to the end of the world.

Christ is with me, what can I fear? Let the waves of the sea and the wrath of the powerful assail me; all of that weighs no more than a spider's web."

True faith is certainty, not doubt. It is serenity, not anxiety. It is joy, not sadness. It is the ability to face the world, because we know we are not alone, that Jesus accompanies us. Suffering, when offered and accepted, has infinite value. It fills us with grace, it purifies us. And when you can no longer bear it, pray with the Psalms. There is so much richness in them. This one in particular (Psalm 27) encourages you to face life's great trials, to overcome your pain:

"The Lord is my light and my salvation, whom shall I fear? The Lord is the stronghold of my life, of whom shall I be afraid?"

With You, Lord, and Your Word, I shall fear nothing.

Intercede for your family, pray for them so that none may be lost. In the end, eternal salvation will be the only thing that matters.

~343~

The year we have journeyed together is coming to a close. It has been a walk that I have enjoyed; has it been the same for you? We traveled together in faith, with a goal, discovering the wonders of our holy religion. Today we will start the day by doing something very special, reconciling ourselves with God. To forgive and be forgiven... there is no more effective balm for the wounds of the soul. Let us become temples of God.

Now, find a quiet place (no matter where you are) and say to the Lord:

"My God, I repent of my sins and I am truly sorry, because I have deserved your punishments by sinning and even more because I have offended You, infinitely good and worthy of being loved above all things. With your holy help, I resolve not to offend you again and to avoid the occasions of sin. Lord, have mercy, forgive me."

God looks upon you at this moment with pleasure. He is happy because you have decided to change. If you listen in your heart, you can surely hear these words from Him: "I am here and I love you. I will give you the grace you need to change. I give everything and I expect everything from you. You are my greatest desire. My greatest joy."

"Lord, I love You. And I ask You to forgive me."

During the week, try to go to a church, find a priest, and make a good sacramental confession. Then, participate in Holy Mass and receive Communion fervently. From that moment on, the world will change for you. You will see everything anew, grateful, with the eyes of Love.

God wants you to be holy. He asks this for a very particular reason: so that you can spend eternity with Him. He knows that life on this earth is too short and longs to have you by His side and give you all His love.

A friend once told me that it is impossible to be holy. We have so many temptations and often fall into them. They think that holiness is something difficult, beyond our reach, something of times past. "These are not times for holiness," they said to me. But it is not true. This is the best time to be holy. The world needs it. God asks for it. And it is so simple to achieve.

~344~

Nothing compares to the purity of the soul. It is the greatest treasure you possess. A sanctuary where God Himself resides. Purity allows you to see and understand many things, because you look at them without pride, with humility and simplicity.

A priest once said in his homily: "Do you want to be happy? Be pure. Look at the children, how they play without worrying about anything. There is purity in their souls." The pure soul is full of God. There lies its beauty. It lives in God. It rests in His love.

I still remember the excitement of a friend of mine who went to confession after many years. He came to work with tears of joy in his eyes. He was happy. "I feel free," he said, unable to contain his joy. "It's like I've left behind a sack full of stones that was weighing me down." He found his place as a child of God, knew himself loved by the Father, and regained the purity of his soul.

I met him again some time later. He still had the joy of that first encounter. "Now I visit Jesus every day," he told me excitedly. "And when I arrive, if the church is closed, I stay for a while, standing at the door, talking to Him."

A holy priest once said, "When our sins prevent us from daring to approach Jesus, we always have Mary. We can confidently turn to her." I have seen it hundreds of times, sinners who have returned to the Father, repentant, thanks to Mary's timely intervention.

"To Jesus through Mary," exclaimed Saint John Paul II emotionally to the youth in Madrid. I am one who goes to Jesus through Mary. In her, I have found the sweet affection of a mother. I sense her comforting gaze in moments of difficulty, and her maternal correction when I need it. We are all sinners. And we fall. But we are also saints in progress. And we are called to spend eternity with God the Father in the Heavenly City. Blessed Sister María Romero said, "We cannot choose our birth, our family, comforts or hardships; not even the years of life or the hour and manner of death; but we can choose our eternity." Strive for it to be a happy eternity. "Would you like to be a saint? Decide for Love? Be holy for God?" “Me, a saint?" "Yes, you, a saint. It will be an excellent life choice." Abandon the sins that drag you down and start walking the path of goodness. Take the hand extended to you by the Blessed Virgin Mary and let her lead you to Jesus. Strive to live in holiness. Guard your state of grace. Do not be afraid.

The next time we meet, I will ask you: "How is that holiness going?" And you, radiant with joy, will reply: "On the way."

~346~

Every morning, driving to work, I passed by the Church of San Antonio. I loved greeting Jesus from the car, telling Him that I loved Him. I continue on my way and make a spiritual communion. This fills my soul with immense joy. In this way, before starting my tasks, I place myself in the sweet presence of Jesus.

A friend does something similar, traveling by bus while praying the rosary. Another friend regularly attends the 6:00 a.m. Mass every morning. We are truly "crazy" in a way. That's why we do things that the world hardly understands. If you think about it, the Gospel seems like madness: "forgive those who offend you, give to those who ask, love your enemy, turn the other cheek." Christians do not illuminate the world with their own light but with the light of Christ, like the moon that shines upon us reflecting the sunlight. From Him, we draw our strength.

An acquaintance once wrote to me complaining, "We Catholics have lost that blessed madness that made us want to set the world on fire with faith and bring the Good News to everyone." I know there are still some of these

"crazy" ones in the world. I remembered a friend who once arrived at my house in a t-shirt, deeply moved. "What's wrong?" I asked him, seeing him in that state. "What happened to you?"
"I met Jesus, poor and crucified," he replied, with a look of immense joy still in his eyes.

I then leaned out from the balcony of the house and could see that poor man wearing my friend's shirt disappearing into the darkness of the night.

A priest recounted in his homily a touching experience. He visited a very poor neighborhood in Guatemala and came upon a house made of zinc sheets. The floor was dirt and they barely had any belongings. In one corner, he saw a woman caring for an elderly lady.

"Is she your mother?" asked the priest.

"No, she's not," replied the woman. "I found her lying on cardboard and brought her to my house."

The priest looked at her in surprise.

"I had never seen her before," the woman continued, "but she is poorer than me and needed care."

Such love and charity! Such a presence of God in her life! What a beautiful way to evangelize, without saying a word, by living the Gospel fully with simplicity and joy.

~347~

Stop searching further. Only God will calm your fears and anxieties, fill your life, and give you the certainty of knowing yourself as a beloved daughter from eternity.

The absence of God is the greatest tragedy of modern man. We live so busy that we have no time to think about eternity. We miss the opportunities that God presents to reconcile with Him. A priest once recounted that he celebrated a Mass for the soul of an elderly man who had passed away. Before giving the final blessing, he said to those present: "I will be available in the sacristy for anyone who wishes to confess. One never knows when God will call them into His presence."

No one came forward. In the afternoon, he received a phone call:

—Father, did you hear?

—No, what happened? — asked the priest.

—When you finished the morning Mass, one of the attendees, an elderly gentleman, suffered a heart attack on his way home and passed away on the spot.

We have so many opportunities in life to earn heaven. Don't let them pass by. Never wait until it's too late to make a good confession.

~348~

You must restore the presence of Jesus in your life, work, and family. Let everything revolve around Jesus. Take confidently the hand that Virgin Mary extends to you. She will lead you to Jesus.

It's sad to think what the Virgin Mary told Catherine Labouré when she showed her the design of the Miraculous Medal. The rays emanating from her hands were the graces she wished to give to her children, but many were lost because no one asked for them. "These luminous rays are the graces and blessings that I expand upon all those who invoke me as Mother. I am so happy to be able to help the children who implore my protection. But there are so many who never invoke me! And many of these precious rays are lost, because they rarely pray to me."

People are hungry for God! And they don't know how to approach Him. They fear doing so. Men think they will lose their manliness. Women are concerned about children, home, husbands, and don't make time for themselves, to care for their souls, to recover sanctifying grace.

It's up to you to bring them a bite of Eternal Love, restore their hope, help them regain inner peace. Guide them to find the richness of our holy Mother Church, under the shelter and protection of the Immaculate Heart of Mary.

No matter how many times you fall in your apostolate, you are not alone. Mary will always reach out her hand and give you the strength you need to start over. Rise up! Trust in Her.

Saint Maximilian Kolbe, the Knight of the Immaculata, left us this spiritual advice: "Never be afraid of loving the Virgin too much. You can never love her more than Jesus." She is our Mother in heaven. Throughout my life, I have experienced her presence and maternal protection. That's why I often advise everyone I can: "In the adversities and afflictions of life, in great temptations, in pain, turn to Mary."

I share with you a beautiful prayer so that you can consecrate yourself to Mary and receive her affection, advice, and protection.

CONSECRATION TO THE VIRGIN

"Oh my Lady! Oh my Mother! I offer myself entirely to you; and in proof of my filial affection, I consecrate to you this day my eyes, my ears, my tongue, my heart: in a word, my whole being.

Since I am all yours, oh Mother of goodness, keep and defend me as your own possession. Amen."

~349~

"Let your fragrance spread like incense, your blossoms open like the lily, give off your perfume, sing a hymn." Sirach 39:14 If today God were to call you into His presence, what would happen? How would He see your soul? It is said that Saint Teresa had the grace to see the state of her soul and nearly died of fright upon seeing a soul in mortal sin. There's a charming anecdote about Saint Dominic Savio. It is said that Don Bosco asked him the same question: "What would you do if you knew you were going to die in an hour?" And Dominic replied, "I would continue doing what I am doing now." Dominic Savio had the serenity of someone who knows they live in a state of grace. That's why nothing disturbs him. And what about me? What should I do? Very simple, renew your life, learn to forgive, set aside the resentment that prevents you from living. God gives the strength for this, and more. If you have the presence of God, you will be kind to others, you will seek their good more than your own, you will help as many as you can, give good advice to those who need it, not remain silent in the face of injustice, not be afraid to speak of Jesus and defend His Church. You will receive graces you didn't even imagine. God is wonderful in this way. He gives you more than you ask for, constantly indulges you, showers you with gifts. And in return, what does He ask of you? To try, to desire holiness, and to pursue it as a life choice. Don't be afraid to be holy!

~350~

A few days ago, I heard about a young man who had a overwhelming experience. He was traveling to Las Vegas. He had been distant from God and the church. Suddenly, the plane entered a storm and began to plummet. The scene was terrifying. Some people were bouncing off the walls of the plane, others were screaming in panic. For some reason, he remained calm, searched for answers within himself, and asked the God of life to allow him to live. Then the situation changed. The plane suddenly regained altitude and completed the flight without further incidents.

He discovered God in the most unsuspected place, an airplane. Now he wants to know Him more intimately, to have a deep and personal encounter to nourish his soul and his life.

Our story resembles somewhat this turbulent flight. It is we who decide our destiny when we go through the turbulence of life.

There are many questions that only God can answer. That is why we search for Him so eagerly. Those who begin their search for God will find peace and serenity at some point to continue the journey. They will become saints, after much walking on the narrow path... like many saints who preceded them. Some, whose names we will never hear, anonymous saints, who were saints for God. Saints who endured everything with humility and patience.

God speaks to us in many ways. We must tune the senses of our soul. Prayer and faith. Then you will hear Him, and you will know that it is Him. Some find Him in silence more easily. A glance from God is enough for them. Knowing Him near. Others find Him through the heart. They have so much love that this love is enough to unite their souls with the Love of loves. Some feel God in the tenderness of a child, or the pain of a sick person or someone in need. They know that Jesus is in them, waiting to be loved.

~351~

God speaks to each of us, with particular affection. He calls you by your name. And He does it so delicately. I remember once, while at university, I was overwhelmed by tenderness. At that time, still not understanding such things, I wondered, "What is this?" I was like the Hebrews in the desert when they discovered the manna. They didn't know what it was and said to each other, "What is it?" We often struggle to recognize a gift from God. The truth is, it was an experience that lasted only a few minutes, but it filled me with great happiness. Rarely had I felt such peace and serenity. The tenderness passed, and I remained there, enjoying it, longing to be in a solitary place to remember and reflect on it. Years later, it happened again. I was driving my car, and suddenly it was there. I recalled the previous experience. Again, I wondered what it was. But this time, something was different: I wanted to know more. What do I need to do to experience this again? Where does this joy come from? I hadn't done anything special. I was just driving, oblivious to everything; I wasn't even listening to the radio. It was futile, I couldn't grasp or see beyond my eyes. But such was the sweetness of the moment, the infinite joy, that I wanted to hold onto it at all costs. Time passed. One day, I began my search for God and along the way, I gathered bits of this tenderness. I now recognized what it was, and why it had happened. The answer had always been close by, and I recognized it as John did when Jesus appeared to them on the shore of the Sea of Galilee: "It is the Lord."

~352~

I have seen that all those in love with Jesus, every soul earnestly seeking Him, writes down their experiences at some point. Not with the intention of standing out among people, as this would pose a great risk of "falling into pride," but for the good that their writings can do. God renews our lives like a potter. Indeed, we are restless clay, hard to shape. Many times He has had to reshape us. But each time, He adds an additional grace to the mix to keep us close, united to Him. There are moments of reflection. It has happened to me. It's when I pause. I take a break in the journey. Tired, like the old sailor who has spent months at sea. And I tell myself, "Enough." I then know that nothing on earth can satisfy my thirst. That's why I go to Mass. I fill my soul with the joy of the Eucharist. And I drink until I am satisfied with the living water that is Jesus. I believe God values these efforts to free ourselves, this spiritual struggle, because it grants an additional grace beyond what we already possess.

In my case, I have come to understand how terrible sin is, that no sin is insignificant. And that, for seemingly small things, we may lose our souls. I see around me how souls live in darkness, which is why I write to you. It is worth fighting and moving forward. Trying. Making good resolutions for amendment. Promising to be better. Keeping hope alive. Seeking purity of heart. Holiness. The presence of God. The God of mercy.

~353~

I find no greater joy in this world than speaking and writing about Jesus. He always finds ways to surprise you. He fills you with surprises and gifts. He is a true friend.

Once I was in line for confession at Mass. I was first in line, with about six people behind me. We were all waiting for the priest to arrive. In that church, you don't see him enter the confessional because he uses a door at the back. You know he's there when a lighted sign saying "confessing" turns on. So, there I was, waiting.

Minutes passed, and still no priest. Then I seemed to hear a sweet voice in my heart saying, "Courage, the priest has arrived." I started to think to myself:

"How can the priest have arrived if there's no one there?"

A lady behind me got annoyed because I wasn't moving forward. She stepped out of line and entered the confessional to the astonishment of everyone waiting. Curiously, she stayed inside, even though the sign was off.

"What is she doing?" I thought.

Ten minutes later, she came out, stopped in front of me, and asked, "Why aren't you going in? The priest arrived a while ago!"

I looked at her, not understanding, and she explained, "The sign is broken!"

More recently, something similar happened again. Jesus is very special. A friend told me:

"I went to a church to greet Him. I walked in a bit distracted, and at the door, I felt something strange. It was a sensation that shook my whole body.

'What's happening to me?' I thought anxiously. 'What is this?'

Then I looked up and saw the altar. The Blessed Sacrament was exposed! They were having Holy Hour, and I hadn't even realized!"

Jesus is very jealous of His love. He wants us for Himself, without distractions, with a willing soul and a pure heart.

The Love of loves reveals itself through love. Because love sanctifies us, draws us closer to the good God, and fills us with beautiful experiences that transform our lives and our hearts. It changes us and fills us with tenderness. As Saint Augustine said, "Love, and do what you will. If you remain silent, you speak with love; if you shout, you shout with love; if you correct, you correct with love; if you forgive, you forgive with love. If love is rooted in you, nothing but love will be your fruits."

~354~

Never doubt it...

God loves you.

~355~

'If you love me, keep my commandments; and I will pray to the Father, and he shall give you another Paraclete, that he may abide with you forever.' John 14:15-16

When I think of a virtuous woman, sweet, kind-hearted, and faithful, my tender grandmother comes to mind. Does the same happen with your grandmothers? Anyone who spent time as a child at their grandparents' house knows exactly what I mean. We were loved, hugged, and spoiled.

Every afternoon, my grandmother would rest and pray the Rosary. Seeing her pray, by her example, now as an adult, I pray it too. I know she had her sights set on eternity, God the Father, the Virgin Mary, St. Joseph, and Jesus.

A virtuous woman reads the Bible, thirsts for God, listens to Jesus, and what the priests tell us about him. This is how they show us the virtuous women of the Bible, starting with the purest and most beautiful, the ever-Virgin Mary and Immaculate Conception.

'But Mary kept in mind all these things, pondering them in her heart.' Luke 2:18

Then there's Martha and her sister, friends of Jesus. 'Mary... sat at the Lord's feet and listened to his word.' Luke 10:39 Can you imagine that privilege? The closeness, being called by name. Seeing him, hearing his voice, being able to touch him, keeping his words. Once I read that the modern woman of our time needs to take breaks. If you want to rest from all the hustle and find peace, look to Jesus, listen to his Word, and keep it in your heart. Where can you see him? He is alive in the Tabernacle. Go visit him. And how do you listen to him? It's very simple, by opening your Bible. We all have a Bible in our homes, many open and dusty, on a wooden stand in some hallway. It's time to read it daily and meditate on his Word. You can start by reading the four Gospels of the New Testament: Matthew, Mark, Luke, and John. They tell you stories about Jesus, from before he was born, his life, miracles, his encounters with people around him, but above all they gather his Words and promises. His words give life. He assured it, and I believe him. 'It is the spirit that gives life; the flesh profits nothing. The words that I have spoken to you are spirit, and they are life.' John 6:63 The experts recommend starting with the Gospel of St. John. There's a beautiful verse where he tells us: 'And the Word was made flesh, and dwelt among us, (and we saw his glory, the glory as it were of the only begotten of the Father,) full of grace and truth.' John 1:14 Recommendation before opening your Bible. Say a prayer, ask God for his Holy Spirit, fill yourself with his grace and love. Now let's start reading the Bible. God wants to speak to us. 'Fill yourself with God, so that you can bring him to others.'

~356~

Today I will trust in God.

Despite everything, even if I don't understand anything... I will trust.

~357~

It happens that suddenly you think God has forgotten you. So many problems surround you and you cannot understand them. You find yourself engulfed in a whirlwind with no apparent way out.

Recently, I went through something similar and felt great confusion. I tried to stay calm and trust in Jesus. I used to visit Him in the Tabernacle to pour out my complaints... And I prayed with Psalm 6: "Lord, do not rebuke me in your anger or discipline me in your wrath. Have mercy on me, Lord, for I am faint; heal me, Lord, for my bones are in agony. My soul is in deep anguish. How long, Lord, how long?... Turn, Lord, and deliver me; save me because of your unfailing love."

At that moment, it was as if an inner voice said to me: — Read Job. — Job? — I said to myself, puzzled. And that's what I began to do, and what I recommend when you don't understand what's happening to you, and when you feel you can't go on.

As I write, I have a Bible open in front of me. It's open to the book of Job. Now it has become a dear friend. It helped me understand the teachings of Our Lord. Who are we to complain before God? Do we think we offer our sufferings for the salvation of souls?

We are not worthy of anything. It is all by the grace of God. Job understood this well:

"I know that you can do all things; no purpose of yours can be thwarted. Surely I spoke of things I did not understand, things too wonderful for me to know. My ears had heard of you but now my eyes have seen you. Therefore I despise myself and repent in dust and ashes." (Job 42:2-6)

You suddenly understand how small and insignificant you are before the immensity and magnificence of God. It's as if God Himself takes you to the limit to test your faith, strengthen it, and make you understand that without Him, we can do nothing. "For as gold is tested in the fire, so those who please God are tested in the furnace of affliction." (Sirach 2:5)

He delights in humble, simple, and upright hearts. And He teaches us to be as He desires us to be.

~358~

You, who receive Jesus in the Blessed Sacrament in your hand, do you realize what is happening? You hold God in your hands. Did you know that the living Jesus is present in every particle? No matter how small it may be. He is there, whole and entire. That's why you must examine the palm of your hand very carefully.

"I am a specialist in the Holy Shroud," wrote to me the renowned Spanish priest, Father Jorge Loring. "I have given over a thousand lectures on it, wrote a book on this topic. And I have attended several International Scientific Congresses on the Holy Shroud. While attending a Congress held in Turin, after the sessions of the Congress, the attending priests concelebrated the Holy Mass in front of the Holy Shroud.

Suddenly, I felt immense emotion being so close to a cloth soaked with the blood of Christ.

My heart was beating strongly. But I thought, 'It is thrilling to be so close to the blood of Christ, but every day I hold the living Christ in my hands during the Holy Mass, and I do not feel this emotion.' It's because we are so miserable that we get used to the greatest things and treat them routinely. Since then, when saying Mass, I try to concentrate on the wonder that I am celebrating."

~359~

I used to work in a company where many people would come. Talking to them, I realized that some carried crosses so heavy, they could barely bear them. Then it occurred to me to cut out little pieces of paper, like doctor's prescriptions, and started giving spiritual prescriptions. At first, they were very simple: "Remember to pray at night." "Be Happy." I would fold the paper and say as I handed it to them: "If I were a doctor, this is what I would prescribe for you." And they would leave happy with their spiritual prescription. Months and years passed this way.

One day, one of the people to whom I had given this prescription returned to the company: "Visit Jesus in the Blessed Sacrament." He was excited, happy, with a smile and a joy overflowing. "I can't believe it," he said to me, "Jesus has changed my life. Now I visit Him daily, and when the church door is closed, I greet Him from outside and spend some time with Him. It's the best thing that has ever happened to me."

I was amazed. And I understood that nothing compares to having an experience with Jesus. My words encouraged them, but Jesus transformed them. Time passed, I left that job, and I forgot about my spiritual prescription pad. I started writing about my experiences with the good Lord, and along the way, we began writing and publishing these books on spiritual growth on Amazon. I could never stop writing. A very sweet voice inside me urges me, "write." And that's what I do. I share my experiences with Jesus, who has become my best friend.

Tonight, while praying, I suddenly remembered the prescription pad and got the idea to write down the top 5 that had impacted their recipients the most in this book. It was providential. In the following pages, you will find these spiritual prescriptions that will do you a lot of good. It's one prescription per page because every day we face different situations. That's life. We never have identical days. These are recipes for the soul. To help you encounter Jesus.

SYMPTOM: I HAVE MANY TEMPTATIONS
PRESCRIPTION: PRAYER. YOU MUST PRAY

Can't stand so many temptations? Do you fall into the same sins over and over again? You lack prayer. Pray. How will you resist temptations if you stay away from God? Prayer is the best defense against temptations. "Watch and pray so that you will not fall into temptation," Jesus recommended us. That's the key to overcoming those tough times. I've had times when I face temptation. In those moments, I remember to pray. Usually, I pray the Holy Rosary. As I pray, peace returns, doubts dissipate, and everything becomes clear. These are moments of peace, of closeness to God.

~360~

SYMPTOMS: OUR APOSTOLATE IS A DISASTER, IT'S GOING FROM BAD TO WORSE.

PRESCRIPTION: HOLY HOUR

I often hear these concerns from various prayer groups and religious associations: "My prayer group is fading away." "No one in our group wants to participate anymore." "We feel the fervor with which we started is dwindling."

The solution is very simple. Practice daily, with deep devotion, the Holy Hour. Spend one hour accompanying Jesus in the Blessed Sacrament every day, knowing that it is Jesus Himself who invites you to be with Him. Saint Peter Julian Eymard wrote: "Consider the hour of adoration you have chosen as a time in paradise: go as though to heaven, to the divine banquet, and this hour will be desired and greeted with happiness. Sweetly hold the desire in your heart. Say to yourself: 'In four hours, in two hours, in one hour I will go to the audience of grace and love of Our Lord. He has invited me, He waits for me, He desires me.'"

I once read that when Mother Teresa of Calcutta began her apostolate for the destitute, she realized the immense needs of the poor. Her first collaborators, seeing the multitude of needy people, said to her: "It's impossible for us. We will never be able to handle this. We are few, and there are hundreds and thousands of dying, sick, and abandoned children." They placed this problem in God's hands and prayed. Eventually, a word came to their hearts: "Holy Hour." They began a daily hour of Eucharistic adoration after finishing their daily work.

She herself said: "In our congregation, we used to have adoration once a week for an hour; then in 1973, we decided to have an hour of adoration every day. The work that awaits us is enormous. The homes we have for the sick and dying destitute are completely filled everywhere. But from the moment we began to have an hour of adoration each day, our love for Jesus became more intimate in our hearts, the affection among us became more understanding, and our love for the poor filled us with compassion, thus doubling the number of vocations. God has blessed us with many wonderful vocations. The hour we dedicate to our daily audience with God is the most valuable part of the whole day."

The result is evident; her congregation spread throughout the world, bringing hope and consolation to the most needy.

What we lack is this: purity of heart. A pure heart to receive Our Lord. To become a Living Tabernacle, where He makes His dwelling. To clothe ourselves with Christ. To be one with Him.

~361~

SYMPTOMS: I FEEL LONELY

PRESCRIPTION: EXPERIENCE THE LOVE AND NEARNESS OF JESUS

Do you feel lonely? You are not alone. Jesus accompanies you. You must learn to experience His closeness, His presence, His love.

Once, I went to a radio program where we talked about Jesus and how He accompanies us, even though we do not see Him. During the program, we received a call from a listener. It was an elderly lady who said excitedly, "I used to be scared of everything. Any noise. Any shadow. I was constantly anxious. Now I am no longer afraid. Nothing scares me because I know I am not alone. Jesus accompanies me and will always be with me."

This prayer has sprung from my heart, and I share it with you: "I am a seed, Lord. Plant me in Your Heart, so that I may germinate and bear fruit."

~362~

SYMPTOMS: I THINK NO ONE LOVES ME, THAT I'M WORTH LITTLE

PRESCRIPTION: VISIT JESUS

I love visiting Jesus in the tabernacle. I know from experience that you receive wonderful graces in His presence. That's why it's my favorite prescription. I don't know anyone who has visited the Blessed Sacrament and remained the same. He tends to transform people. He fills them with peace and gives them hope. He listens to them. And He reminds them how much He loves them.

Knowing that we are loved from eternity is the most wonderful thing that can happen to us. It's like silently approaching the tabernacle and hearing a sweet voice coming from it saying:

"I am. And I love you. You are precious in my eyes."

"But Lord," you respond, "don't you see all the bad in me?"

And He, gently, will say to you: "Despite everything, I have never stopped loving you."

~363~

SYMPTOMS: I'M OVERCOME BY ILLNESS

PRESCRIPTION: OFFER IT TO JESUS

Offer your illness to Jesus. Sometimes illness brings us closer to Him. We unite our sufferings with His and help save countless souls.

I heard about this priest who was suffering from a terminal illness. Every day he united his sufferings with those of Jesus. And this saintly sick person would say: "How good it is, now all I have to do is suffer for Jesus."

No one wants to be ill, but when it comes, we can give it infinite value. Jesus will know how to reward us for this surrender.

We must accept God's will, even if we do not understand it.

This is perfect joy:

Accepting everything. Offering everything. Abandoning ourselves in His Love.

Let us pray...

Soul of Christ, sanctify me.
Body of Christ, save me.
Blood of Christ, inebriate me.
Water from the side of Christ, wash me.

Passion of Christ, strengthen me.
O good Jesus, hear me.
Within Thy Wounds, hide me.
Suffer me not to be separated from Thee.

From the malignant enemy, defend me.
In the hour of my death, call me.
And bid me come to Thee.
That with Thy saints I may praise Thee.
Forever and ever.

Amen.

~364~

SYMPTOMS: I FEEL THAT JESUS IS CALLING ME AND I DON'T KNOW WHAT TO DO

PRESCRIPTION: BECOME A LIVING TABERNACLE

Do you feel that Jesus is asking something of you and you're not sure what it is? It used to happen to me. As a child, what I wanted most was to be holy, to make Jesus happy. As an adult, that longing continues because Jesus has kept this love alive, this need to have Him as a friend. Jesus is my best friend. I love saying it, talking about Him, writing about Him in my books, telling everyone about Him. And I do it with excitement. "If people knew you better," I tell Him, "they would never turn away from you." You must remember that Jesus is truly there. Become a living tabernacle. Bring Jesus to others. Many people need a friendly voice, a hug, to know the love of Jesus. How to do it? With a clean soul (everything is resolved with a good confession), living in His presence, keeping God constantly in your heart, with fervent and frequent communion. And every time you pass by a tabernacle, in that special moment, remember these words: "There is Jesus, He sees me and He hears me." Then kneel down and tell Him you love Him. "Jesus, I will always love you."

Believe it, you're an incredible woman!

Would you like to write to me? Here is my email address: edicionesanab@gmail.com

May the good Lord guide your steps, protect you, and bless you always.

~365~

What a wonder! We've reached day 365.

You have no idea how excited I was thinking about this day, what it means, or how happy and proud I feel of you. I know it hasn't been easy, and for you, a virtuous, brave, and empowered woman, it's an extraordinary achievement.

I see you like a mountaineer who manages to climb a mountain with a very steep slope and plants her flag at the summit. But this time, you did it with Jesus. Together, you climbed God's mountain.

We stand before His presence, grateful for so much love. There's so much more I have to share with you for your well-being and spiritual growth. So many experiences.

I thought a lot about which story to use to close this chapter of your life, and I remembered one word: "Trust." They say mothers have an intuition that lets them know when something happens to their children. I was at my son Luis Felipe's school when a teacher approached me. "Mr. Claudio, I need to tell you what happened to me. I read a lot of your writings and books. You insist that we should trust, that if we trust everything will be fine. Last Sunday, I was in my apartment when I felt that something bad had just happened to my daughter. It was a feeling of terror. Instantly, the phone rang; it was the building concierge. 'Your daughter was hit by a car outside the building and is lying in the street.' I took the elevator down and ran to her. My hands were shaking uncontrollably, and I couldn't dial my cell phone to call an ambulance. At that moment, I remembered your words and said to myself, 'Trust. Everything will be okay.' And I started reciting this ejaculation: 'Jesus, I trust in you.' I regained my composure, called emergency services, and the ambulance arrived. My daughter is fine now and wanted to thank you." Her story surprised me. "Let's thank Jesus," I told her.

This year, God asks us to trust, despite everything and against all odds. And just in case there were any doubts, on Monday I read St. Faustina Kowalska's Diary, I opened it, and this is what appeared before my eyes:

"The graces of My mercy are drawn by means of one vessel only, and that is trust. The more a soul trusts, the more it will receive. Souls that trust boundlessly are a great comfort to Me, because I pour out all the treasures of My graces upon them. I rejoice that they ask for much, because it is My desire to give much, very much. The soul that trusts in My mercy is the most fortunate, because I Myself take care of it. No soul that has called upon My mercy has been disappointed or brought to shame. I am particularly fond of the soul that trusts in My goodness."

I believe He is also asking this of you: "Trust." I will spend time asking Him to teach me to trust, like a mother teaching her child to take their first steps. That's how I want God to teach me, knowing that He will be there if I fall, to lift me up and embrace me. "Lord, I love you, teach me to trust, fully, lovingly... in you."

I learned to trust in Jesus, to love Him more. I knew I was loved by God, what more could I ask for? I trusted Him with the simplicity of a child. That's why whenever someone came to me with a problem, I sent them to Jesus: "Go, go to the Tabernacle, Jesus is waiting for you there."

Everyone returned amazed and told me, "You should publish what happened to me in one of your books. I can hardly believe it!"

This is what I always do when I have difficulties:

- I trust.
- I pray.
- I visit the Blessed Sacrament frequently.
- I make a good sacramental confession and continue to confess frequently to maintain grace in my soul.
- I try to attend daily Mass to receive communion and have God's presence in my life.
- I seek advice from a priest as a spiritual director.
- I read the Bible.

In complicated cases, it is advisable to seek prayer groups to pray for your intentions. I have witnessed the power of prayer, especially when others pray for you. I discovered this recently and was impressed.

I have learned three things in life:

1. God will never give you a cross heavier than you can carry. It's a safe path to heaven.
2. God cannot be understood. I've spent years wondering why many things happen. And to this day, at 66, I still have no answers. I came to the conclusion that God doesn't need to be understood; we simply need to trust because everything that happens to you will be for your good. Surrender to His love. Serenely accept His will because everything He does is out of love.
3. This is the most important thing of all: Knowing that we are special to Him. He loves us very much. Like His favorite children. I experience this daily. And I know it's true.

Now I bid you farewell, only for the moment. I hope my book has been a great blessing to you. Pray for me, I pray for you. Do not be afraid. Trust. And God will do the rest.

God is good.

CONCLUSION

A few days ago, I listened to Randy Pausch's lecture, a professor at Carnegie Mellon University. It's titled "The Last Lecture," and in Randy's case, it was true because at the time of delivering his lecture, he was dying of cancer. He had a beautiful family; his children were young, and during his talk, which lasted nearly an hour, he never complained. He never shouted. He never cried. He simply said, among other things, always smiling: "I'll be like Tigger, the friendly and innocent tiger, friend of Winnie the Pooh. Live cheerfully, full of optimism. I'm going to be happy for the time I have left."

Millions of people have watched his video on YouTube. It's truly inspiring. "The most valuable thing we have," Randy said, "is time. What do we do with our time, our life's time? We value it so little, and in the end, it's the only thing that matters."

Randy was right. I've decided to enjoy life more, complain less, strive harder to achieve my dreams, seek God, read the Bible, live sacramentally, and take care of my family. I wanted to share this with you.

I've thought about how we waste our lives, savoring resentments, hatreds, living not to hurt others or indulge in pleasures. I want to be different. I've set myself to see more sunrises, enjoy more with my loved ones, help anyone I can, and trust in God. And share my experiences with you. After all, time does not belong to us; it's His, and although we may want to prolong it, we can never achieve it. What will you do with your life?

If you ask me if you are special to God, I would answer without hesitation: "More than special. You mean everything to Him. And He loves you infinitely." And if my words don't convince you, or what I say, I would refer you to the Holy Bible, the one you have at home. Look up "Isaiah 43" and start reading. #If you cross the river, I will be with you and the current will not drag you away. If you walk through the fire, you will not be burned, nor will the flame scorch you. For I am Yahweh your God, the Holy One of Israel, your Savior. To save you, I would give up Egypt, Ethiopia, and Saba in exchange for you. Because you are precious and honored in my sight, I love you, I would exchange people for you, and nations for your life."

God has a mission for you. He has entrusted you with important things... He has placed them in your hands...

Sometimes I place a small table with my books at the exit of a church. People of all ages approach to browse the books and converse. For some reason, they tell me their concerns and problems. I speak little and listen attentively. More than once, they have told me surprising stories: A mother's love, a woman's heroism. The deep pain of a grandmother left alone. I admire women's ability to carry such heavy burdens and dedicate their lives to others. They ask little for themselves and give everything. I couldn't resist expressing my admiration in writing. I sat down to write, and thus this book was born. I dedicated it to my wife, Vida, who has "put up with" me all these years. And boy, has she been patient! It's not easy to live with someone as absent-minded as me. Life isn't simple. It deals blows that hurt. But it also gives us hopes, joys, and dreams. It's up to you what to choose. I choose hope.

I love thinking: "How good God is."

The Pope has written that women make the world more beautiful, protect it, and keep it alive. I believe him. A new and wonderful world awaits you. Now, it's up to you. Imagine what we could do as Catholics living our faith fully... The world would be a different place. And so would we. I believe we would have the courage to live the Gospel. Forgive. Love. Trust. Leave the ties of this world and truly be free.

The years have passed, and now you feel that nothing is the same. Life's blows have led you down another path. I have learned that with Jesus, everything changes. No one remains the same in His presence.

You have the opportunity to correct your mistakes. And save your soul for Eternity. Yes, this is the best moment of your life. When you can say to Jesus, "I want to be yours, let my life belong to you." And by His grace and love, you will be.

The world needs to regain its hope. Hope is what gives life meaning. Hope is like literature because it opens up new worlds and possibilities. You can't buy it, touch it, or sell it... It grows, spreads, multiplies, and helps you improve as a human being. It gives you prudence, strength, helps you be enterprising, and fight for your ideals. It allows you to dream and pursue your dreams. With hope, you can generate prosperity. It restores your dignity as a human being. It motivates you to study, read, strive, work, and be happy.

So, I wish you hope, that you become happy again, that you don't be discouraged by the blows life often deals you. Cheer up!

IMPORTANT

If you enjoyed this book, please take a few moments to write a review of it. I'd really appreciate it.

Review this product

Share your thoughts with other customers

Write a customer review

Did this book help you in some way? If so, I'd love to hear about it. Honest reviews help readers find the right book for their needs.

Hey...

The day is here! My book, "365 Daily Devotionals for Women", is finally live on Amazon.

I have one simple ask:

If you were able to look at the book and enjoyed it, can you leave a short review?

First find the book on Amazon. Go to the site where you purchased it and scroll down until you see the "Review this product" button. Click on the button and you will go to the Customer Review Page. Click on it and follow the steps. It's very easy!"

Reviews should only be 1-2 sentences and should take about 30 seconds to leave (and would make a huge difference for me). If you can't come up with one, here are some examples:

- **It is a book that fills the soul with joy, 100% recommended.**
- **I have enjoyed reading these meditations.**
- **A beautiful, mystical journey through a Catholic lens.**

Thank you all for your support!

Thanks so much for your help! I can't thank you enough.

Best,

+Claudio de Castro

Contemporary Catholic Writer

The Catholic Author Claudio de Castro has published other books on personal development, spiritual growth, and self-help similar to this one that may interest you. They are available on Amazon and are very easy to find. Simply go to Amazon and type "Claudio de Castro English Books" in their search bar, and they will appear ready for you to choose the one you like the most. Here are a few suggestions for you to appreciate.

THANK YOU FOR SUPPORTING OUR APOSTOLATE OF THE WRITTEN WORD.

CLAUDIO DE CASTRO
UNVEILING THE
SECRETS OF
HELL
TESTIMONIES OF THOSE WHO
WALKED THROUGH FIRE

The
MONK
HABITS
for Everyday
Applying the Spirituality of a
Benedictine Monk to our daily lives
Best-Selling Catholic Books
Claudio de Castro

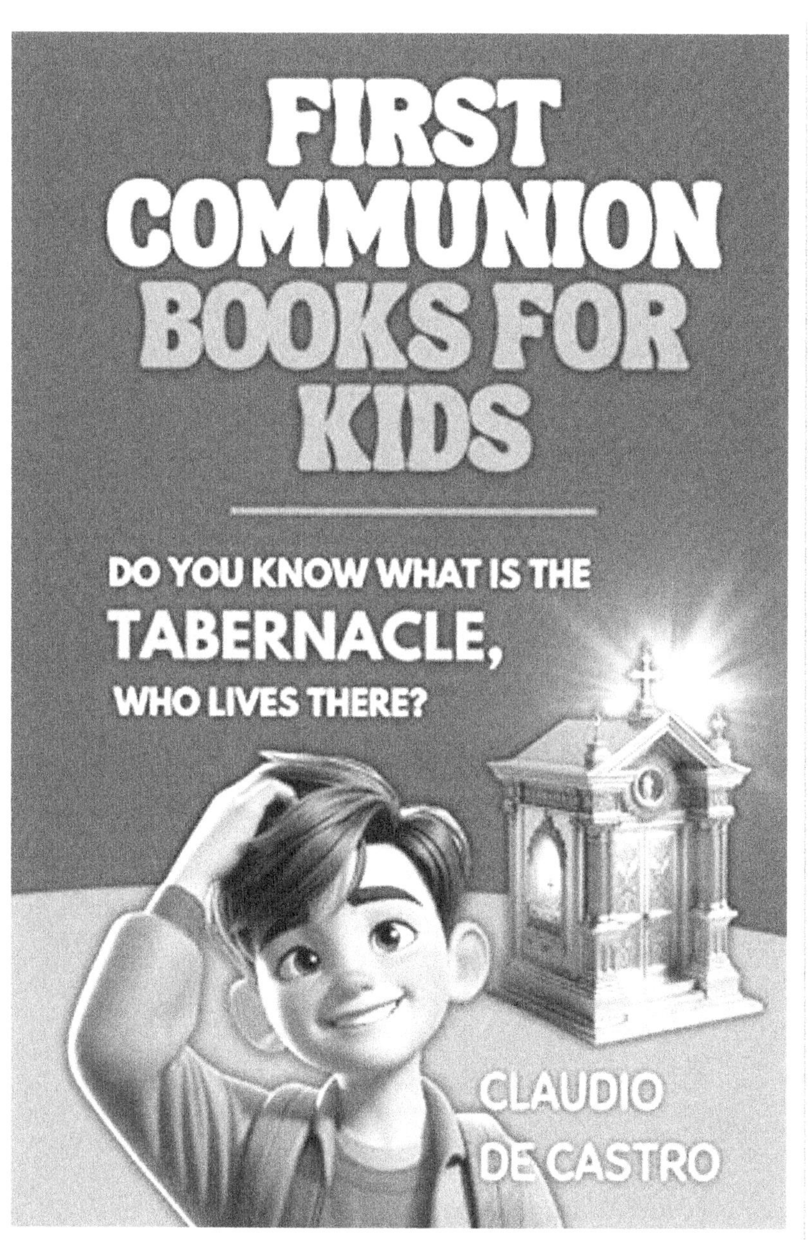
FIRST COMMUNION BOOKS FOR KIDS
DO YOU KNOW WHAT IS THE
TABERNACLE,
WHO LIVES THERE?
CLAUDIO
DE CASTRO

Printed in Dunstable, United Kingdom